MW01116004

Connecting The Current

A Treaties on Consciousness and Greater Mysteries

By Cal Melkez

ASTRAL MIND FOUNDATION PRESS

Copyright © 2024 by Cal Melkez, All rights reserved

All rights reserved. No part of this book may be reproduced, distributed, or transmitted in any form or by any means, including photocopying, recording, or other electronic or mechanical methods, without the prior written permission of the publisher, except in the case of brief quotations embodied in critical reviews and certain other noncommercial uses permitted by copyright law.

Publisher: Astral Mind Foundation

First Edition, 2024

Disclaimer:

The information provided in this book, *Connecting The Current: A Treatise on Consciousness and Greater Mysteries*, is intended for educational and informational purposes only. The practices, techniques, and rituals discussed herein are based on historical and contemporary spiritual practices.

Cal Melkez and the Astral Mind Foundation disclaim any liability for any direct, indirect, or consequential damages or loss incurred by individuals using or relying on the material contained in this book. Readers are advised to use their discretion and judgment in applying the information provided and to seek professional advice when necessary.

By using the information in this book, the reader agrees that Cal Melkez and the Astral Mind

Foundation are not responsible for any adverse effects or consequences resulting from the application of the methods and practices discussed. This book is not intended to replace professional medical, psychological, or legal advice. Always consult with a qualified professional before undertaking any new spiritual or health-related practices.

About The Author

Cal Melkez is a renowned spiritual life coach and Reiki master, whose expertise in astral projection and magic has guided countless individuals on their paths to spiritual awakening. With a background in psychology, Cal brings a unique perspective to understanding human consciousness, integrating scientific principles with ancient esoteric knowledge. For over a decade, he has dedicated himself to teaching the transformative practices of meditation, astral projection, hollotropic breathing, transcendental meditation, and ritual magic.

Cal is the host of "The Astral Mind Podcast," where he delves into the intricacies of astral travel, kundalini awakening, and the profound benefits of connecting with higher spiritual realms. His engaging teaching style and deep insights have earned him a loyal following on platforms such as YouTube and TikTok, where he shares techniques and wisdom to help others unlock their full potential.

In addition to his online presence, His innovative system of Astral Cord Tethering offers a revolutionary approach to connecting with the spiritual realm, providing readers with the tools to harness their innate magical abilities.

Cal's mission is to awaken people to their highest potential, guiding them to explore the vast possibilities of the mind and spirit. Through his teachings, he continues to inspire a global audience, helping individuals transcend their limitations and achieve profound spiritual growth.

Foreword

Mysteries of Consciousness

In the vast expanse of human history, there has always been a relentless pursuit to understand the deeper truths of existence. From the earliest shamans who traversed the spiritual realms to the modern-day mystics exploring the frontiers of consciousness, this quest for knowledge has remained a constant. It is this journey into the unknown, this search for the divine within us and the universe, that forms the heart of *Connecting The Current: A Treatise on Consciousness and Greater Mysteries.*

The Hidden Truths of Magic

Magic, often relegated to the fringes of superstition and folklore, holds profound secrets that transcend the material world. The rituals, symbols, and practices detailed in this book reveal a world where thought and intention can shape reality, where the boundaries between the physical and the spiritual blur. This is not mere fantasy; it is a rediscovery of ancient wisdom that has been systematically obscured throughout the ages. The truth of magic, as you will uncover, is not only real but accessible to those who dare to seek it.

The Power of Astral Cord Tethering

Central to this work is the revolutionary system of Astral Cord Tethering. Passed down through esoteric traditions and now revealed in its entirety, this method allows for a profound connection with the spiritual realm. By tethering one's astral body to higher energies, practitioners can unlock immense potential, gaining insights and abilities that were once the exclusive domain of mystics and sages. This book meticulously guides you through the process, ensuring that you can safely and effectively harness this power.

Ancient Wisdom

Throughout these pages, you will encounter the wisdom of ancient cultures, from the mystical traditions of Egypt and Sumer to the esoteric practices of the East. These traditions, long hidden or misunderstood, offer a roadmap to spiritual enlightenment and personal transformation. By integrating these ancient practices with modern techniques, you will be able to tap into a reservoir of knowledge that spans millennia.

The Council of Light

At the heart of this spiritual journey lies the Council of Light, a collective of enlightened beings who guide and support those on the path of awakening. This council, which includes deities such as Shiva, Odin, and Thoth, represents the pinnacle of spiritual evolution. Their teachings, now made accessible through this book, offer profound insights into the nature of reality and the cosmos. By connecting with the Council of Light, you align yourself with the highest frequencies of divine consciousness.

An Invitation to Transformation

As you delve into *Connecting The Current: A Treatise on Consciousness and Greater Mysteries*, you are not just reading a book; you are embarking on a journey of self-discovery and empowerment. The rituals and meditations within these pages are more than exercises; they are keys to unlocking your true potential. Whether you seek to connect with spirits, enhance your magical abilities, or simply understand the deeper truths of existence, this book offers a comprehensive guide to achieving your goals.

May this book serve as a beacon of light on your path, illuminating the mysteries of consciousness and revealing the boundless potential within you. Embrace the journey and let the wisdom of the ages guide you to a higher state of being.

Table of Contents

Connecting The Current

Introduction

It's an impossibly daunting task to distill into palatable form one's experience of enlightenment, and to even do so, in one manner or another, is to dull the blade. I, like you, have a destiny to live out, a purpose predetermined for me. That is, if I choose to walk it. You see, this work stands as a testament to the ever-present necessity of participation in this game of life. Throughout this book I will introduce many topics that haven't ever been expressed in written form, some traditions that have remained in obscurity, hidden from the modern world since antiquity. I must share this information because I was blessed to do so. And do so, I must. I am not trying to convert you or convince you that the way I see the world is right, or anything close to it. To do so would rob you of the very reason for your decent into this reality. To rob you of experience is the duty of modern structures of trust and blind obedience. No. I can confidently say we've been denied this most necessary of human rights. It's time now to reclaim the freedom that was so cunningly stolen from us. I'm not here to lay out a path for you to follow. Simply put, that's not my place and the task would be wildly redundant, if not merely pathetic. My goal is not and very will be to define a path for people to walk. Not now. Not ever. A path is not what true seekers of truth actually need. If this book has found you, regardless of the connections, it's because this book is meant to liberate you from the limitations you've put upon yourself. It is meant not to lead you down a path you've never known but to unveil the path that is more real than even you.

At its core this book seeks to reveal the hidden esoteric meanings of ancient texts and spiritual practices to shine light on lost teachings used to connect with the divine. Foremost, this book will address what the path is and how one reaches it. This book is difficult. The concepts and ideologies presented will test and stretch your perception of yourself and the world around you. It is my sincerest hope that despite the challenging nature of these ideas, you discover the link between yourself and the divine.

In this work I will share methods and techniques used to make contact with deities and use a form of magic that is vastly different than the ones widely used. I discuss enlightenment, how it feels, what it looks like, and how one might reach that state. Most importantly, why it's crucial that you enter this state of being and persist steadfastly within it thereafter. During my time with my reiki master, I found his most defining trait to be his connection with others, established through the vessel of storytelling. Those experiences he shared with me strengthen my faith and gave me the fuel needed to press on when the answers seemed impossible to find. Following that example, I've fashioned this book with my life experiences woven into the pages.

Hidden in Plane Sight

To most people's surprise, spiritual texts weren't ever meant to be taken as literal physical fact. Which is why evidence of historic events from mainstream religion isn't there. In a world of physicality, it's easy to cast literal meanings on symbolic texts meant to enliven the spirit. But one thing is sure, of the varies stories told through history about gods and men, the central purpose has always been to guide man back home, often leaving a path behind for others to follow.

We're in a period of awakening characterized by an unprecedented access to knowledge, where ancient texts, once the guarded secrets of sages and scholars, are now available to anyone with the curiosity and the will to seek them out. The nature of magic, once dismissed by the rational mind, is being reconsidered as a legitimate field of study, intertwined with the spiritual beliefs that have guided humanity through the ages. As science continues to achieve breakthroughs in energy and our understanding of physics, it also illuminates the mysteries of the soul and metaphysics, bridging the gaps in our understanding of both realms.

The Pursuit of Magic

Magic, in the most basic sense, is the art of influencing the unseen forces that shape our reality. More precisely, it is the practice of tapping into the hidden currents of the cosmos, aligning oneself with the universal laws that govern existence, and channeling this energy towards specific outcomes. Throughout history, magic has been both revered and feared, its practitioners often walking the fine line between enlightenment and heresy. Yet, despite the attempts to suppress or control it, the knowledge of magic has persisted, passed down through generations in whispers, symbols, and cryptic texts.

Man's pursuit of magic can be found throughout the beliefs of all ancient cultures. It's not too much to say magic is here because man is here. For instance, civilizations that predate recorded history, such as those in Mesopotamia, Egypt, and India, developed sophisticated spiritual systems that incorporated magical practices. These early societies understood that the material world was but a shadow of a deeper, more profound reality—a reality where spirits, gods, and unseen forces played an integral role in the unfolding drama of human life.

Magic Throughout History

To truly grasp the influence and present-day importance of magic, one must dive into the rich history of ancient cultures and uncover the mysteries left behind. One of the more recurring myths in the ancient world is the mystery of advanced beings visiting ancient civilizations. Interestingly, these stories share outstanding similarities despite cultural bounds. Among the most enigmatic of these visitation accounts are the tales of the of Atlantis and the lesser-known northern land of Thule pronounced Too-Lee. While Atlantis is widely recognized through the writings of Plato, who described it as a powerful and advanced civilization that sank into the ocean in a single day, Thule remains shrouded in even greater mystery. Mentioned by ancient Greek explorer Pytheas and later by Roman historians such as Pliny the Elder, Thule was described as the highest point of the known world, a land where the sun never set and the boundaries between earth, water, and air blurred into a mystical haze.

However, to view Atlantis and Thule purely as physical locations is to miss their deeper significance. These legendary lands are allegorical, representing states of higher consciousness and spiritual enlightenment. Take Plato's allegory of the cave and the symbolism it used to express freedom from limited perspective. In the same way Atlantis symbolizes the zenith of human potential and the subsequent fall from grace due to hubris and moral decay, a theme echoed in many religious and mythological traditions. Thule, on the other hand, represents the quest for ultimate knowledge, a spiritual ascension beyond the physical limitations of the body into the realms of the divine.

Taken as purely physical, the stories of these advanced civilizations scarcely make sense at all. And science swiftly does away with their faulty logic, missing the deeper meaning. The allegory of Thule is particularly poignant in the context of magic. In this narrative, Thule is not merely a distant, icy mountain but a place within each individual where the elements of earth, water, and air meet. The earth symbolizes the physical body, grounded and tangible, the water represents the astral echo, fluid and ethereal, and the air represents the domain of the gods, subtle and boundless. The journey to Thule is thus an inward voyage, a process of transcending the material world and connecting with one's spiritual double. It is a journey that requires courage, dedication, and often divine intervention.

Ancient texts such as The Epic of Gilgamesh, the Bhagavad Gita, and many others tell the story of celestial beings who live atop mountains guiding and communicating with those who would eventually achieve enlightenment. This usually resulted in the birth of the religions seen today. These guiding spirits are believed to have fashioned the universe and continue to impart their wisdom to humanity. Throughout history, figures such as Jesus and Buddha have been guided by these very spirits, receiving divine insights that have shaped the spiritual landscape of their respective cultures.

The Inner Summit

The quest for the inner summit and connection with the divine is not a journey that can be taken lightly. It requires a deep understanding of the ancient teachings and the ability to navigate the astral realms. This book aims to uncover the hidden connections between various spiritual traditions, demonstrating how they all tell a story of divine intervention and the possibility of magic through the use of spirits.

Whether you are a seasoned practitioner or a curious seeker, this book offers something for everyone. It is an invitation to explore the depths of your own being, connect with the higher realms, and awaken to the magic that resides within you. Together, we will uncover the secrets of ancient spirit magic and learn how to harness its power for personal and collective transformation.

As you read, I encourage you to keep an open mind and heart. Allow the stories and teachings to resonate with you on a deeper level. Reflect on your own experiences and how they connect to the themes explored in this book. Most importantly, remember that the journey to enlightenment is a personal and unique path. Trust in your own inner guidance and the support of the divine beings who walk with you. The meditations, rituals, and philosophical views expressed in this book will remind you that the journey is possible and that you can take a moment to rest without losing progress. For indeed rest is the state were intuition flows freest. The ritual provided below is intended for anyone new or experienced in the practice of magic. This ritual aims to imbue your book with magical properties, making it a conduit for good fortune, health, and spiritual contact. The book will act as an amplifier for manifestations and spiritual abilities, ensuring that the blessings of the Council of Light are bestowed upon the reader every time they open or touch the book. This ritual can be performed at any time but works best when done before reading any further, as it serves to awaken you as you read. Whenever you choose to use this ritual, it will be potent and lasting.

Blessing of the Council of Light

Materials

Connecting The Current

- Your book
- Four candles (white)
- Incense (frankincense or sandalwood)
- A small bowl of water
- A small bowl of salt
- (optional) Images or symbols representing the Council of Light (Shiva, Odin, Thoth)
- (optional) A clear quartz crystal

Preparation

1. Choose a quiet, sacred space where you will not be disturbed.
2. Arrange the four candles at the cardinal points around your workspace.
3. Place the book in the center of your workspace.
4. Light the incense and let the smoke purify the space.

The Ritual

1. **Creating the Magic Circle:**
    - Stand in the center
    - Point your finger at the ground and slowly rotate clockwise, visualizing a protective circle of light forming around you.

- Say: "By the power of the Omnium Current and the light within, I create this sacred circle, a space between worlds."

2. **Invocation of the Elements:**
    - Facing east, light the white candle and say: "I call upon the element of Air, bring clarity and wisdom to this space."
    - Facing south, light the white candle and say: "I call upon the element of Fire, bring passion and transformation to this space."
    - Facing west, light the white candle and say: "I call upon the element of Water, bring intuition and healing to this space."
    - Facing north, light the white candle and say: "I call upon the element of Earth, bring stability and strength to this space."
3. **Invocation of the Archangels:**
    - Facing east, say: "I call upon Archangel Raphael, guardian of the east, protector of this sacred space."
    - Facing south, say: "I call upon Archangel Michael, guardian of the south, protector of this sacred space."
    - Facing west, say: "I call upon Archangel Gabriel, guardian of the west, protector of this sacred space."

- Facing north, say: "I call upon Archangel Uriel, guardian of the north, protector of this sacred space."

4. **Invocation of the Council of Light:**

    - Place your hands over the book and say: "I call upon the Omnium Nexus, the divine Council of Light. I invoke thee, Shiva, lord of transformation and cosmic dance. I invoke thee, Odin, seeker of wisdom and keeper of runes. I invoke thee, Thoth, master of knowledge and scribe of the gods. Infuse this book with your divine energy and blessings."

5. **Consecration of the Book:**

    - Sprinkle a few drops of water on the book, saying: "By the element of Water, I consecrate this book."
    - Sprinkle a pinch of salt on the book, saying: "By the element of Earth, I consecrate this book."
    - Pass the book through the incense smoke, saying: "By the element of Air, I consecrate this book."
    - Pass the book over the flame of each candle, saying: "By the element of Fire, I consecrate this book."

6. **Charging the Book with Intent:**

- Hold the quartz crystal in your hands and visualize a bright, white light emanating from it.
- Place the crystal on top of the book and say: "This book is now a doorway for good fortune, health, and spiritual contact. Every time it is opened or touched, it amplifies the manifestations and spiritual abilities of the reader. The blessings of the Council of Light are upon this book and all who interact with it."
- If you do not have a crystal, simple imagine a ray of pure white light shining down on the book, purifying and charging it with divine energy.

7. **Affirmation and Oath:**

    - Place your hand over your heart and recite: "I, [your full name], stand before the Omnium Nexus, pledging my dedication to the path of light and wisdom. I vow to honor the teachings of Shiva, Odin, and Thoth, and to uphold the principles of the Omnium Current. May this book serve as a beacon of light and power to all who seek its guidance."

8. **Closing the Circle:**

    - Thank the deities and the elements: "Thank you, Shiva; thank you, Odin; thank you, Thoth. Thank you, elements of Air, Fire, Water, and Earth. Thank you,

Archangels Raphael, Michael, Gabriel, and Uriel."

- Use the dagger to symbolically cut through the circle, saying: "I release this circle, but its protection and energy remain with this book. So mote it be."

9. **Integration:**

    - Sit quietly for a few minutes, meditating on the energies you have invoked and feeling the connection with the Omnium Current.

    - Say your own personal prayer of intention to signal the end of the ritual.

By performing this initiation ritual, you align your book with the ancient energies and wisdom of the Omnium Nexus, making it a powerful tool for good fortune, health, and spiritual contact. Every time the book is opened or touched, the reader will receive the blessings of the Council of Light, amplifying their manifestations and spiritual abilities. And with that, let us begin.

Chapter 1

The infinite Path

Two long years of searching and longing finally brought me face to face with what I had been hoping for. The saying "be careful what you wish for" flittered in my mind as the encounter began. It was far more visceral than I had expected. Everything was real and intense and, to be honest, far more frightening than people had let on. After two long years I had finally done it—peered beyond the veil between this world and the next. I had become Alice falling down the rabbit hole, only I had been falling from the start. I should give a bit of back story about this event to give you a better idea of the level of this accomplishment I had made. At least at the time I thought it was something momentous. Later I realized the experience should be as normal as waking up in the morning. More on that later. To put things mildly, I was overjoyed. Finally, after so long I had gotten another notch on my spiritual belt. From that moment on my spiritual life was my own, not subject to a religious belief or cultural opinion. I had truly experienced something life changing. And though naïve the thought, it was a step in the right direction. There will come moments in everyone's life where they must decide to embark on their own journey or forfeit their story to be a side character in someone else's.

For those who don't know and have sadly never heard, we are more than our physical bodies. And thanks to near death experiences and the effects of DMT on the brain, science is discovering that consciousness doesn't originate from the brain but is an extremely sophisticated receiver of a radio signal. To fully experience this, we'll have to look at a number of phenomena pertaining to how consciousness and the perception of reality can be augmented. The most accessible of these phenomena is Meditation. I know you've heard of this before, but I challenge you to approach this discussion from another angle. You may be familiar with Vipassana, the style of meditation that suggests focusing on all incoming stimuli in an effort to quiet the mind so that one can reach an altered state of consciousness. If you prefer to look at things from a strictly scientific view, like myself, you'll see that what we determine to be reality is in large part the result of our perception at any given time and that has to do with the many influences we face. Mediation is one such powerful way to augment the way we see reality.

But what's the point of all this discourse on the mind's mailability? As stated earlier, my goal is not to provide to you a new path you haven't heard of. The aim of this work is to reintroduce you to the truest of paths leading to that ever so elusive state of connection one experiences when in relation with divinities. Some would argue quite adamantly that the purpose of our time here on earth is to reach enlightenment, samadhi, or nirvana? The first of the challenging concepts one should understand as they set out to discover the connection to concrescence, is that words are the filter of human experience. By use of words we can describe something in fine detail, yes. But at the same time the very thing one may describe is nothing at all like having the actual experience. It is a symbol referencing the tangible.

The futility of human language to describe the totality of an experience can be easily seen when one tries to describe a psychedelic experience. The moment someone embarks on an exploration of mental freedom, they realize upon their return the profound lack of resources they have to accurately map the terrain of that mental dimension. Some people after the consumption of high doses of psilocybin report that they weren't in this reality at all, having been transported to a strange new reality where everything is connected, both people and nature. If nothing else, such experiences suggest the mind has capacity to transverse such obscure dimensions.

The Depths of Reality

So, if the mind is able to produce strange and unbelievable effects through the use of psychedelics, that reveals there is more to reality than what we can perceive. Let me stop you there. A unwarranted leap can be made here. One can think that the perception of reality is all there is, and in part be correct. The danger comes when one thinks any rendition of reality is accurate. This is why science is a such a valuable resource. We need a medium by which we can all reach the same bases of understanding. Through this book I'll be talking about some very "far out" topics like paranormal activity, ESP, and other mystical buzzwords that cause ears to perk. Before I dive into that kiddy pool, I want to establish that I'm not crazy and that you have good reason to keep reading this book.

Beyond The Physical

With that said, let's start with the basics. As I've stated, you are more than your physical body. I wholeheartedly believe this. You will also have to come to a place of wholehearted belief based on your experiences. All that I've learned over my 15 years of spiritual searching, angelic visitations, teachings at the feet of my guru, Astral Projection is the most direct way of experiencing that. If you've never heard of the term, it can mean many things to many different people. How does this relate to connection and concrescence? We're getting there. Don't worry. Astral projection has been around for as long as people have been writing about the sun and moon. You can find depictions of astral travel in Egyptian text and just about every indigenous culture. For the longest time, however, it's been something that was kept hidden from the general populous, reserved for the especially spiritual among us.

The History of Astral Travel

Astral projection, the ancient art of soul or consciousness traveling outside the physical body, pervades numerous cultures and religions throughout history, each imparting a unique narrative of this profound experience. This enigmatic journey transcends the physical realm, touching the core of spiritual practices and beliefs about life and the afterlife across civilizations. In Egyptian tombs, astral projection is whispered amongst the hieroglyphs. The Egyptians called it "ka," a traveler's twin that roamed the realms of gods and the dead. Their Book of the Dead is replete with spells and rituals to guide the ka through the Duat, or the underworld, reflecting a meticulous understanding of out-of-body experiences as a journey towards immortality.

The ancient Greeks also spoke of soul travel. Plato, in his myth of Er, narrates a soldier's spiritual journey after death and his return to his body, bearing wisdom from the beyond. Similarly, the practice of "ecstasy" in Greek mysteries, such as those at Eleusis, hints at a form of conscious separation, where initiates perhaps ventured beyond their physical confines to grasp divine truths. In the spiritual culture of India, astral projection is an intimate thread within Hinduism and Buddhism. Known as "Sukshma Sharira" or the subtle body in Hindu texts, it is a vessel for the soul to journey through various planes of existence. The ancient yogic practice of pratyahara, or sensory withdrawal, sets the stage for deeper states of consciousness, where one may experience astral travel and accessing realms described in the Vedas and Upanishads. We'll talk more about the importance of sensory deprivation in later chapters.

Connecting The Current

Astral projection can also be found among the shamanistic traditions of indigenous cultures worldwide, from the Americas to Siberia, are perhaps the most vivid and enduring practitioners of astral projection. These shamans, or spiritual healers, traverse spiritual worlds, communicate with spirits, and retrieve wisdom and healing for their communities. Their journeys, often induced by rhythmic drumming or entheogens, are not merely for personal enlightenment but are integral to the social and spiritual fabric of their cultures. Astral projection can be found in the Islamic world as well. Sufism, with its mystical teachings, embraces the concept of "soul travel" or "miraj," reflecting the Prophet Muhammad's own nocturnal journey where he traveled spiritually to the heavens.

The Age of Knowledge

Fortunately, with the advent of the internet, the creation of forums, and almighty YouTube, occult knowledge is freely available to anyone and everyone whose interested. Depending on who you ask, astral projection can be the act of one separating their spirit from their body, projecting a double of themselves into the world around them, or the ability to move their perception of reality to a different location. Regardless of what you believe astral projection is, it hinges on the idea that you can experience reality beyond the confines of this physical one.

Long before I became an astral projection coach, I was an obsessed researcher on the topic of astral travel. I remember many late nights reading articles, browsing through forums, and practicing techniques to no avail. Chances are you're just like me. You've been practicing a spiritual technique, adhering to a strict routine to better yourself, and been observing all the popular self-help best practices. On the hierarchy of difficulty, you may have in your mind that enlightenment is the final and most important goal, taking years to achieve, and that done only by the masters and those who have dedicated the better part of their lives to the pursuit. This, I must confess, is absolute malarky. That mindset is the very reason why the task of connection with source seems so difficult to achieve and why so few achieve it. The proceeding chapters of this book explain in depth how one actually makes connection, and you will find that anyone and everyone can experience the fullness of enlightenment.

Revelations of Consciousness

So, there I was, having finally astral projected after several years of waiting. Looking back, though I hated the period of searching, it was the waiting that truly changed me. You've heard the sayings 'trust the process,' and 'The journey is more important than the destination,'. If at some point those quotes have irritated you, you're in good company. Many people I teach tell me it's hard to trust the process and enjoy the journey, if not totally impossible. Why? Because sometimes the journey sucks. Plain and simple. It's as if problems are an immutable part of the path. When starting a business, the road to financial freedom is tough and few find true lasting freedom. If you've ever tried going to the gym to get in shape, you probably know how difficult it is to stay motivated. But the truth is you grow more on your path up the mountain than you do on its summit.

Why all the confusion then? If the journey is supposed to be the fun and enjoyable part, why even care about the goal? That's exactly the point? Here in lies the paradox of life. What most people desire is the end result, the fulfillment of delayed gratification. "What's the pay off," they ask. This mindset is a perversion of life's purpose. Take music for instance. You don't listen to music just to get to the end of the song. If you listen to music like that you probably need to listen to something else. In western society we've convinced ourselves that nothing matters but the end result, thus everything we do is expected to be painful and arduous, especially the things of most value to us. This often leads people to avoid the perceived difficulty and hardship of chasing after what they really want. Worse still, culture conducted in this way casts a melancholy shade over the importance of the present moment.

Such a revelation about the underpinnings of reality can lead to a feeling of nihilism. Why bother? This was much the same place I was in when I started my spiritual journey. Its natural for these feelings to accompany you as you set out on the infinite path. When I was a child I felt isolated. Nothing felt real to me. I had done all this human stuff before. Birthdays, family outings, celebrations, holidays, nothing mattered because I had done it all before, and many times at that. If you suffer from the reincarnation belief as I do, you may have felt the same during your formative years. I felt as though there was a veil over the world, and I wasn't seeing what lie beyond, though

I could feel the impressions. An observed life in this fashion, without the proper direction, leads to resignation from the human experience. All that apathy led me on a collision course for something more meaningful. That something turned out to be the mysterious existence of the paranormal. As a child I always felt that something was off. As Morpheus describes in the mind-bending film, The Matrix, it felt like an itch in the back of my mind that I couldn't scratch. It was always there; the stalking question: "is this it?", which was quickly followed by the epiphany that plagued the philosophers of old, "there must be more,".

These inquiries into the nature of reality led me first to human consciousness and the power of the mind. Throughout high school I spent more of my time studying the strange and obscure than on the obsessions of my peers. Movies like The Matrix painted this picture that there was something wrong with the world, that we needed to wake up from this endless dream. I believed this because once I looked closely enough at the overlining patterns scattered over the established symbols of the world, down to the trustiest expressions of the universal mind, I found that, no matter how I looked at it, this simply couldn't be the real world. It was just a game we were all living in and had just forgotten we pressed start and created our character. It wasn't long before I learned about hypnosis and the mysteries surrounding the subconscious mind. I knew that within my subconscious mind hid the answers to all of life's questions. This innate knowing led me to many important revelations, and with time and trust, your inner wisdom will guide you all the same.

My studies of self-hypnosis eventually led me to the practice of dream yoga, and to put it mildly, I was obsessed. That so much so because I had finally found something real, or at least the after image of things real. Every waking moment was filled with reality checks, journaling, practicing, and reading the accounts of others. Lucid dreaming was one of the first tastes I had of a reality apart from the waking world we know. Then there was the world of spirituality. I was seduced first by Buddhism and followed the teachings of a guru on YouTube. If you think the hunt for enlightenment began there, you're wrong. The hunt for enlightenment began the moment I realized there was something wrong with the world, that what I was seeing could be all there was. My admission to myself that I wasn't satisfied with life was my first step on the infinite path. In reading this book, confessing to yourself that there must be more to life, is where you currently stand. That's the whole reason for the game, you see. It's pointless to wear robes and shave your head to be spiritual. There is a good reason for it, but without the experience of the revelation, it's fruitless. More on that later.

Though I didn't know I was chasing connection, I could feel the longing for something guiding me on down the path. I wanted to do whatever it would take to uncover the secrets of reality and I was convinced religion held the answers. So, I indoctrinated myself, abiding by all the dos and avoiding all the don't until I again felt something real among the tired husks imitating truth.

As a teenage Buddhist I happily spent a large majority of my time meditating. I was a very lazy kid so any sort of practice that involved sitting was right up my alley. I realize now as I'm writing this that spiritual people must have a tendency to regard themselves as extremely important, much like Clark Kent, a superman hidden in plain sight. This was my disposition, and for the most part that isn't so wrong to think. We are all, for lack of a better term, gods. Well, I guess I could have found a better term to describe that, but I like stirring up conflict where it seems needed.

I knew back then that there was more to me than could be seen. I knew I had the ability to transcend this reality because my home was rooted in another. The only problem was I didn't know how to do that. The dangerous thing about spirituality is that religious leader and gurus of every kind will tell you they have the magic formula to wake you up to your inherent godly nature. They'll promise their technique is the best or their god is the one and only, and we know how the latter goes. My point is, you can get trapped looking for the right key to a door that is already open and can not be closed. If someone means to give you quick solution that promises instant breakthrough, run. What you want is the path.

The Unclutch Breath

Regardless, I believed the hype and tried just about every mediation technique I could find. None of them seemed to get me past the wall of incessant thought that constantly presented itself, that is, until I learned to unclutch from my thoughts. Because I love techniques and methods for experimental purposes, I'll be describing lots of "how tos," throughout this book to allow you the chance to see if any of this nonsense makes sense. The first of them is the unclutch breath. The origin of this technique isn't as important as it's result. Following the instruction from my YouTube guru, I got into a ridged lotus position that was supported by a whole couch of pillows and began to focus on my breathing. Now, I know what you're thinking. You're thinking "Cal, everyone knows you have to focus on your breathing in mediation," And you're right. Everyone knows that. But that's not the good part. Many people know the importance of breath, but few know how to truly use it. The guru told us once we were in a calm meditative position, we needed to focus on the space between our breath. When you do that something rather interesting happens. Focusing on the space between breaths, the moment your inhale flips over to an exhale, has the effect of quieting your mind in a unique way. By focusing on nothing rather than your breathing, you lose track of who you are, hence the name, the unclutch breath.

After a few minutes of this new meditation technique, I began to feel the ground shaking. My first instinct was there's an earthquake happening. Not likely in the Chicagoland area I lived in. But it felt so real. So much so that I started to panic. It felt almost like the ground would give out and I would fall through the world and stop existing all together. It was so peculiar that I forced my eyes open to gain my bearings. However, when I opened them I saw a room that was violently shaking. My heart fluttered at the sight. The rumbling of my perception only lasted a short while then subsided.

The results from that meditation were the reinforcement I needed to dig deeper into my spiritual pursuits, which eventually led me to lucid dreaming and astral projection. It's normal to wonder what the actual difference is, especially if you're looking at it apart from lore. We'll dig into that in a later chapter. My pursuit of the two terms landed me in a bit of trouble, however. Lucid dreaming was the easier of the two to research and practice. So, I found myself practicing every night multiple times a night. Until I was having several lucid dreams a week. As I spent more time in this second world, I came face to face with the dark parts of my mind, the places where light never reached. And much like the bottom of the ocean, the creatures in the depths of my mind weren't very friendly. It was as if my explorations of my dream mind somehow opened a door to real spiritual interactions.

That was around the time I learned about sleep paralysis. If you've ever had the misfortune of waking up while in sleep paralysis you know just how terrifying it can be. Despite the obstacles sleep paralysis presented, I found myself embracing it and over time learning to stop it in its tracks. Eventually I came to accept that sleep paralysis was the product of a deep trance, something I didn't fully understand at the time but could feel was crucial to the process. It wasn't long until I was practicing self-hypnosis and trance induction, eventually leading to the night of my first astral projection experience. As many of those nights went, I meditated several hours before bed. That day I decided to listen to binaural beats during my meditation, following the suggestion of a forum post. Several hours after that meditation session I set off to bed. While drifting off I did the self-hypnosis technique I had been practicing. It involved focusing on the blackness of my closed eyelids for fifteen seconds, then listening to the fine sounds in my ears for fifteen seconds, and then focusing on any and every bodily sensation I could feel for the same amount of time. I did that whole routine 4 additional times or until I was sleepy enough to drift off.

My First Out of Body Experience

Later that night I was startled awake by a nightmare and found myself lying in bed soaking from sweat. When I regained myself, I tried getting up only to find that I was violently immobilized. I say violently because it was different than the usually sleep paralysis I had come to know. This paralysis was accompanied by strong feelings of vertigo and inertia, it felt like I was on the giant drop at Six Flags Great America. It felt much like the sensation one gets when they are about to crash their car, that impending momentum. It was terrifying. And the longer it went on the more intense it got. I truly felt as though I was dying. I even said to myself "if this keeps up, I'm going to die," and I believed it. Never had I felt anything so powerful. I know now that this is referred to in the new age community as vibrations.

When I had finally reached my limit and could take no more, I felt someone grab my shoulders and pull me out of my bed. The sensation was like none other. It felt like I was pulled out of myself, like a snake shedding its skin, all the while a buzzing, tingling sensation enveloped me. It finally stopped when I was on the floor next to my bed. I got up rather confused as to what the hell was going on. My confusing compounded when I looked down at my bed to find myself still laying there. That was my melting mirror, my white rabbit leading me to wonderland. From that moment on, nothing in life mattered more than the freedom that astral projection offered. I didn't know it then, but my astral echo (the astral body or double) pulled me out of my body and initiated that experience. I'll talk more about the astral echo in a later chapter.

The Road to Enlightenment

Enlightenment, as it's presented today, is the promise of freedom from the confinement of society, from the mediocrity of normal life. I mean who wouldn't want to wake up knowing they were somehow inherently special. This may seem like common sense, but everything in life tells us we aren't special and that we need something external to use to bring lasting and abiding happiness and fulfillment. Can you be happy in every moment? of course not. But that's all a part of the journey that we're supposed to be enjoying, remember. You may read my astral projection experience and think that's amazing and long to experience that yourself, and that's fine. That's just missing the point. The reason I share that story is to express that there is in fact more out there, and like any hero's journey, you must be awakened from complacency into action. The best way I know to do that is by sharing with you how a normal guy like myself has lived through some very abnormal events, some you would hardly believe. I am no more important than you are. In fact, no one is. We are all just people. The moment you realize the journey isn't to a mountain top but to the center of your being is the very same moment you'll realize enlightenment isn't something you reach, it's something you are. That's the big secret, you are already enlightened. You are already connected to source. But you may be thinking, "Cal, don't be silly. I'm not enlightened." I'm not surprised you feel that way. After all, everything in media, music and literature tells you that enlightenment is a crescendo of trumpets and heavenly choirs. There are times when divine beings pay you a visit but when you're awake to your godly nature, these visitations will be commonplace.

Naturally, you'll have to climb the mountain to truly see that it is, after all, just a mountain. I don't intend to rob from you the fun of venturing forth to discover yourself and grow. That is after all the reason why this whole game was created by 'insert deity here'. It is my sincere hope that as you read this book, you'll come into contact with extraordinary forces and have amazing experiences that help you navigate through the different realms of this thing we call life. Therefore, we must embark on this journey together, not to find enlightenment or its derivatives, but rather to the infinite path inward.

Connecting The Current

Chapter 2

The Nature of Connection

You can't reach God. Let's face it. It's not going to happen for you. You don't know God and you are not meant to. A rather intimate relation is made between knowing and reaching that most miss. Many parade around in linen garments with sparklers and censers, claiming to know God, ever boasting of their ability to present you with a path to reach source. With sure resoluteness I can affirm that none of them know God. Those who faint knowledge, know the very least. The concept that most of the modern world holds about God is a perversion, a dilution of purity. In that sense, your god doesn't exist. Now before you resolve to burn this unholy book, let me explain why that is. I said in the previous chapter that enlightenment isn't something that can be obtained, just like being human can't be obtained. Naturally, it is an act of futility. It is simply something that isn't possible when you look at the logic of it. Let's dissect the notion itself—Reaching God. To reach for something in this figurative sense means to strive to achieve, gain, or possess that which is not currently in possession, which remains at distance or beyond physical attainment. The very verbiage of this makes connection with God sound like a prize to be won or a trophy to raise high above the heads of defeated contenders. However strange that analogy may sound to you, there is a striking truth buried in it.

The Spiritual Arena

Many view life as a type of competition. If you asked your neighbor what animal is the king of the jungle, they'd invariably say the lion, or the more accurate would say the human animal. Concerning this point I'm about to make, there are a lot of peripheral ideas that must be addressed. Let's first tackle the kingship that is implied when people mention lions. The lion is the king of the jungle, why? When you think about it that is a very compelling question. There are many creatures in the jungle that are greater in strength than the lion. If you don't believe me, take a look at the elephant. Or better yet, present to the lion an alligator, a beast of two terrains, capable of maneuvers the lion couldn't dream of matching, and adorned with thick armor-plated skin. If one were to watch the animal planet or a British nature documentary, they would very quickly see that, though the lion is formidable, it is not infallible and can be bested by many other creatures in its kingdom.

So why is the lion regarded as king? Was there an election? Or perhaps a succession of royalty? No, I don't think that's the case. Lions hold the title of ruler for the obvious cinematic meaning we've given it, but there is something deeper at play. The lion is a contender. The lion claims the territory as do the apex predators of other terrains. So, the first point I want to make is the necessity of the contender. Reality is like an arena, but what is an arena without gladiators, crowds and judges. This goes back to the idea of the cosmic play we see in Hinduism. Everyone has their roles that they must strictly adhere to. The lion's role is that of the predator, the competitor. The role of the predator is one of challenge. In any pursuit or championship there are competitors contesting for the prize, whether it be riches or glory. This is done in the contest of life. We as humans have taken every area of life and made a competition of it, a contest of champions, where there is only one victor and many losers. There is no sense of growing or advancing together. There are some that would say this is the way of life, why fight it, and that may be true. But with our advanced minds and capabilities we should strive for a greater result.

Business is the obvious arena of money and success, but it isn't the only one we see in our modern world. The minds of man are teeming with competitions and rivalries. Whether it be school, play, or passion, we've made a society where there will always be a winner, which implies there will always be a loser. Where then does enlightenment fit into all this? Enlightenment is just the game that people play when they've grown tired of the rat race of society. Many think to venture into the world of spirituality is to find themselves, or be free, as if there was someone to find and something to get free from. It certainly may feel like there is, but I assure you, it is just a game we play to amuse ourselves.

Controlling the Inner World

For instance, in order for someone to start their spiritual journey they must first accept that they do not have within them the very thing they are searching for. They must acquiesce that they have no value until things are gained. This, if you look closely, is the core of every adventure video game out today. You must find what was lost or never had to best some tyrannical lord or save the clumsy princess. In either case, you must go on a hunt. So, before we go on any further, I must say again, you will not, cannot, and must not reach God through the means offered in this world. Real magic requires a movement away from physical limitation. Striving physically to manifest your desired reality or encounter ascended beings is futile without the etheric counterpart.

Manifestation and the different methods of manipulating reality will be talked about later in this book, but for now I want to explain how connection and manifestation are one in the same force, two sides to the same eight-sided dice. If you will for a moment, think of connection with God as a dream, just as the philosopher Alan Watts suggested. In lectures he would tell his audience to conduct a thought experiment where they believed they were able to dream and control the entirety of their dreams. Naturally one's mind goes to hedonistic things first, which Watts took into account. It is to be expected that once you can control your reality that you will pursue the pleasures within it. He then went on to tell them that they would naturally get bored, as we humans do with anything we have complete control over. In response to this natural progression of boredom he suggested that one day you'd say to yourself, "let's have a dream that isn't under control," the thought being that something would happen to you, and you wouldn't know what to expect. Then the thrill of not knowing would swiftly return.

This daring exploration of self would eventually lead you, after many outrageous and unforeseeable events, narrow escapes, and near brushes with death, to the very world you live in now, having made life difficult and unforgiving, unpredictable and unyielding, just the way you like it. You see, life is a game. This whole experience of duality, individuality, pain and suffering, is the result of your desire to experience something new. And if you were to think a little deeper into this thought exercise, you'd find that Watts was referring to the creator, which of course is you. The more you think about it the more you'll find it makes sense.

If you've ever played a card game or solo game for long enough, you know you can get bored with it rather quickly. This is why video games are designed with levels of ever increasing difficulty to keep you entertained. Hidden in this analogy of reality there is further truth: You must therefore be the creator of your reality and the experiencer of it simultaneously. Let's say you could control your life and make it whatever you wanted. It would end with you eventually relinquishing control so that you could experience the world you've created. You'd have to.

As an artist I know the challenge of creating art that I can't appreciate as much as someone outside of me will appreciate it, because they are separate from me the creator, making them the perfect experiencer. When I write, I know I won't ever read the writing the same way a reader will. If you want, try to see the universe in the same way, like a dream that is under you control. Only now your subconscious mind, the universe, God, source consciousness, or whoever you want to call it, created this reality and the many that flow in and through it. It also created you, a version of itself that could experience the grandeur of creation without the eyes of the creator, so that what was created could be appreciated in its entirety. That is, with the eyes of a child.

Intrinsic Connection Within

If you search deep within, you'll find that you were born connected with the divine. I don't blame you if you don't believe that. Everything in our modern world denies that fact. So, let me explain. What is enlightenment to you? Is it a guru sitting atop a mountain, isolated and stoic? Or is it perhaps the holy monk? Whatever your idea of enlightenment is it hinges on the idea that to be enlightened, you must either possess a command over reality, or reach a level of transcendence above it that you can no longer be bound by its laws, able to see past it to the realm eyond. If that's what you think of enlightenment, ou're not right and you're not wrong. Consider this. nlightenment is both the process of achieving and the ause of the pursuit. One cannot search for God ithout already being connected to God. To truly nderstand unadulterated connection, we must talk bout enlightenment in greater detail.

m certain you've built up in your mind an amazing nage of what enlightenment is. As stated earlier, you ave been indoctrinated by pop culture to see nlightenment as Neo breaking free of the Matrix. But ou fail to realize this is only a step in the right irection. Let me tell you why enlightenment isn't what ou may think it is. The unfortunate truth is nlightenment is hard work. Not the hard work of the lesh but of the mind. The type of hard work that isn't lashy or impressive and goes unnoticed by the natural vorld. So then, why would the conventional belief bout enlightenment and connection with source be een as impressive? Why would it be a surprise to view n amazing awakening moment as just that? It's not ard to be impressed by the obvious, and ostentatious lisplay of the extraordinary. Ultimately, it's not hard o glorify the glorious.

'ou've likely heard the saying, the greater the effort he sweeter the reward. It doesn't just mean the things f physical toil but also of things mental. With that in nind, look again at enlightenment. Is it not easier to iew enlightenment as something godlike and etheric nd powerful, much like Neo in the matrix? Now let me sk you, which is harder? To marvel at the Grand Canyon, or to be awestruck by a blade of grass? Seeing

as the difficult things yield more benefit, you must se
it is the mundane, the average, and the ordinary thin
that yield the greatest reward. In his letter to the
Corinthians, Paul says of God "He chose what is foolis
in the world to shame the wise; God chose what is wea
in the world to shame the strong;" It must then be the
things hidden in plain sight that reveal the deepest
mysteries.

With that in mind, try to see enlightenment from a different perspective. It isn't the transcendental experience of rising above reality. Rather, enlightenment is seeing that reality in and of itself is transcendental. It's realizing that the monk and the guru are worshipers of life itself, lost in a dance of perception, the ever-changing canvas of reality. This o
course isn't easy to do. Finding the beauty in the basic
is an act of wizardry. We all would much rather be carried away into another reality, lifted under arm by angelic beings to learn of our divine nature. But something in that must imply the need for the opposit
the need for the ordinary.

The divine blueprint from which we were created is often portrayed as foolish and weak. This often overlooked internal realm is the most mundane and natural. We all daydream and exercise our imaginatio
muscle. From little steps does come great things. Spiritual breakthroughs of significant magnitude come
from observance of the subtle aspects of reality. The ancient texts of the Sumerians and Akkadians tell the
story of other worldly beings that imparted power into
the DNA of man. On the surface these are stories abou
the creation of humanity. But with a careful eye the

esoteric story can be uncovered. These ancient texts are telling us that we are infused with divine genes. Within us is a storehouse of power than can be used to alchemically turn base metals to gold, to turn physical matter into etheric. That's the nature of connection.

Enlightenment is the realization that you need not do anything to achieve this. It is the easy and free understanding that you already are at the finish line. When I started to interpret the sacred texts allegorically, I began to see that the infinite path began with inner enlightenment and that connection with god begins in the kingdom of heaven found within. I mentioned earlier that enlightenment and manifestation were closely linked. Manifestation, many would agree, requires a clear understanding of what you want and the belief that you can have it. Sure, there are other tools one can use to negotiate with the universe, but I'm not concerned with that now. My aim is to show you the power that simple belief and will have over your reality.

You control your outer world by controlling your inner world. What you put into your mind is what you will see in the world around you. It's as simple as that. The mind is like a field, and you are the farmer. You can plant in your field seeds of positivity and life, or seeds of negativity and death. Both will yield abundantly more than what was sown. This applies to every area of your life. Think, therefore, about the pursuit of enlightenment. The very verbiage used implies you don't have it. If you put in your mind that you don't possess a thing and must go after it, in many cases tirelessly, that is what will be produced in your life.

You will strive and struggle to achieve something you already have. You are the sleeping God, the dreaming creator, who has forgotten who they truly are and so tortures themselves unknowingly.

This idea that you are insufficient needs to be done away with. Put plainly, you need to unlearn it. Society will tell you that you don't have enough, and you need to buy this product, or that you need this car, or that you must wear these clothes to be respected. Since a child you were taught to seek and want and long after things you don't currently have. This disparity is the very reason we as humans have such a rough go of life, unable to be at peace like our animal counterparts. We stress and worry over the affairs of our lives, wanting and needing more to feel valued. The path to liberation from this sad outcome is to find your value internally. This is the goal of meditation, to understand on a deep level that you are as necessary as the stars and the planets that circle them.

True Awakening

Many of us are desperate for freedom from a way of life that doesn't fulfill, and if it does, not for very long. We want lasting happiness, connection with the earth and our purpose. There is a place you can go to be free from the stress and constant pain the mind feels. That place is the heart. We live to much in our heads. And, no, I don't mean to ignore reason or abandon scientific scrutiny where appropriate. What I mean is to wake up. I know this phrase is rather ambiguous. "Cal, I'm already awake." I know. But you aren't. Not really. You are still dreaming. You still think that to wake up means to open your sleepy eyes and stretch off the dreamworld. No. Waking up doesn't even mean realizing you are in a dream. Waking up means putting down the ego you've created to navigate that dream. It means to approach life without the filter of judgment you've put on it and to just experience it. When you can finally just take life as it is, apart from how you think it should be, you'll be free from the prison of your mind.

It is the condition of fear and regret that steals our energy. Many of us spend our time not in the present moment but trapped in the past or in an imagined future. When we divide our energy up between our past and future we leave very little energy, if any, to the present, the only real thing that we experience. In case you were unaware, the only thing that ever exists is this moment right now. This moment you are reading this. Nothing else exists for you but this moment. Anything else that happens in your mind takes you away from what's real. That goes for your perception of reality as well. Chances are you wouldn't know enlightenment even if it hit you in the face.

Enlightenment is about returning to yourself. It's about pulling your mind from the past and the future and bringing it back to the present moment, because you are the present moment. Just as I stated earlier in this chapter, you create your reality, just like the dreamer who created theirs. You are at the center of this experience you are having. You are just as much the experience as you are the experiencer, because one implies the other. You can easily at this very moment feel enlightenment. You can have your enlightenment experience right now. Nothing is stopping you but you.

Nothing is stopping you but the sense of challenge. Because like the lion, you are a contender, and a challenger competing for the crown. You've turned enlightenment into a trophy instead of what it truly is.

Like every other area of life, the spiritual mountaintop we call enlightenment has been turned into a competition, another kind of rat race. Many people who seek it are deluding themselves by thinking they are in some way better than the rest of the world that doesn't seek as they do. I was one of such people. This view, however, is short sighted. In your attempt to achieve, you miss the point. There is nothing to achieve. Many of us struggle through life to achieve titles that ultimately don't matter. If reality is some kind of game, as we will discuss in later chapters, then all that we do here is little more than leveling up a character.

So, I implore you, stop trying to be the king of the jungle, the greatest, or the most renowned. Just stop trying to force the world to look the way you want it to for a moment. Instead, spend your time not being anyone. Take some time to experiment with being no one. Try to put down the mask you've fashioned to do your dealings in society and just allow yourself to be unrestricted by judgment. If you can manage to let go of your filters on life and accept its potency, what you'll find is a freedom that you once had. And in that moment, you may think you've found something that was lost, but, in fact, you've only taken off the blinders from your eyes. You've woken from the self-induced dream, where status and prestige meant something, where your life held no value beyond money and position. You will then see that you were the competitor, the competition, and the judges all along. The moment you stop playing the game and allow yourself to be, is the very same moment you will know enlightenment.

Chapter 3

The Prison Without Walls

What then is the solution to our entrapment in this matrix of our minds? Is it so simple to say the answer is to forfeit? Often when someone hears that they should dedicate themselves to meditation on the present moment, it is met with abhorrence. This is a natural predicament because we think that the solution to our problem must be hidden somewhere beckoning us to find it. This, as I've been stating, only perpetuates the lack within. To truly understand how to free oneself from the shackles of the mind, one must first study the bars that entrap them.

This reality we live in is a matrix that draws its energy not from body heat but from thoughts and emotions. The emerald tablet would call this cage we live in the prison without walls. The idea here is that the only way to trap a god is to make that god believe they are already trapped, or better yet, make them forget they are a god, able to write their lives as they see fit. That is what society is designed to do, make slaves of gods. Corporations and governments draw their power from the people in the same way the machines in the matrix drew their power from the body heat of humans. Now don't mistake me, I'm not saying that infrastructure in and of itself is bad. There are positive benefits to living in society, namely the ease of acquiring food without having to hunt or grow it yourself. What I'm saying is we've been brainwashed to believe we aren't the gods we really are.

This way of thinking supports the capitalistic system we find ourselves in. It doesn't help the system to teach people that happiness isn't something you buy or something that comes from a trip to Hawaii, although those things would be nice. The longer you believe you need to go somewhere or meet someone special to reach enlightenment, the longer it's going to take you to actually "reach" it.

The Prison of Religion

When I was younger and going down the road of a super religious Christian kid, I ran into this exact problem. I was always looking for the next mission trip to go on, the next conference to go to, and the next church service to attend. It became a dangerous cycle of seeking with no result in sight. I remember one night sitting beside a fireplace with some fellow fanatics of the faith as we sang and played guitar. All to the effect of setting the stage for something supernatural to happen. I called it courting the holy spirit at that time, a phrase I had learned from my charismatic mentor. I'll talk more in-depth about summoning spirits and connecting with divinities in a later chapter. It's a topic that can lead to a fair bit of confusion unless care is given to your internal landscape. Suffice it to say, we wanted to connect with God in the usual ways we did.

This time, however, I wasn't my usual enthusiastic self. I was tired. Tired of seeking, of asking, and of knocking with no answers. I began to think to myself, "Maybe god just isn't interested in what I've got to say. Or worse yet, there was no god to be interested in the sad prayers and hopes of a naïve child." Before coming to this realization and weathering the mental storm that comes when one tries to navigate away from religion, I was devoted. I was wholeheartedly seeking. 7 days a week you could find me in a church studying scripture, praying and worshiping. I was seeking something that never made itself known. I was seeking shadows in the dark.

Anyone who would call themselves a Christian, or anyone with strong religious beliefs, probably knows how it feels to fall away from their faith. I went through repeated cycles of falling away and running back to the faith. Why? Because I always noticed that what I was looking for wasn't in the book I was reading or the god I was serving, and it wasn't in the world beyond the church walls. Of course, it wasn't. What I was seeking was a reminder that I was the creator experiencing life through the creation, the aperture by which the universe perceived itself. I was looking for the key to true connection with God, not empty hymns and collection plates. The teachings were devoid of the substance I was looking for. The hidden symbolism of the bible was never revealed.

The Religious Agenda

Let's talk then about Jesus, as he can be found in many ancient texts besides Christianity. Jesus is such a deep topic that a whole chapter in this book is dedicated to who he truly was, his origins, and the magical teachings he left us with. If the name Jesus makes you squeamish, I'm speaking directly at you. Jesus incarnated, as is commonly believed, to show us how to love ourselves, others, and God. Whether you think he will return to cull the righteous and burn the wicked, is beside the point. First and foremost, he came to teach us how to love because love is a much higher vibration than those we experience normally. But this doesn't explain why the religious authorities of his day wanted him dead. The real threat to the structure of power was what Jesus was telling people about the nature of who they were. He told people they didn't need a church to connect with God, but that god was closer to them than their breath.

For centuries the church has had a monopoly on connecting with God, receiving and interpreting his messages. Conversely, if everyone had as much access to God as the pope or priest did, of what value would they be? If people don't need a guide to God, what good is religion. You can see how having someone come in saying they are God and you are too would be bad for business. This is the exact situation we find ourselves in when talking about enlightenment.

How to Free The Mind

Being held in the prison without walls means you are trapped by belief and nothing is actually holding you back. Beyond the physical prison of the body there is nothing to stop you. And due to our naturalistic views of the world, it's hard for many of us to imagine life beyond our bodies. Which is what I want to address. You think you need to be enlightened because you believe you lack something, and as I stated in the last chapter, you are manifesting greater lack by believing you lack something. It's best to just forget and be in the moment because that's all there really is anyway.

So how do you free your mind from this imagined prison? Simple. Stop thinking about it. It's foolish to think any amount of thought would cause you to suddenly arrive at the door to your cell with key in hand. You've been thinking all your life about what makes you happy and what doesn't. That's not the answer. You must simply stop trying to find the answer. I know it sounds horribly counterintuitive, but I assure you it's the answer, if it can be said to answer anything.

The best practice I've found to facilitate this abandoning of effort is the practice of mindfulness. We've already talked about my first experience of mindfulness or letting go. But that in itself is an abstraction of the original technique. Mindfulness has been called by many names and given just as many methods to reaching it. When all you actually have to do is become aware of the moment. This is where the magic happens, or rather where the magic is always happening. I talked in the last chapter about how our energy is wasted between worrying about the past and fearing what's to come in the future. This is true also for our awareness. At any given time, you are simply not here. You are off imagining a future outcome of your efforts or stuck in the past, remembering at 3am, like me, something embarrassing you did when you were younger. The point being you are not here. Take for instance the daydream. When you're in that fantasy world where are you? You may reflexively say you are sitting or doing whatever you were doing before the daydream started. Let me offer you another perspective. You were in both places, the imagined world and the real world simultaneously. In fact, you exist in several worlds all the time.

Let me ask another question that may at first glance seem strange. How do you know you are alive? You could, like the famous Descartes, believe that because you think you exist, however, this line of thought lends itself to the problem of insanity. Those who see the world as a permanent illusion don't think properly and wouldn't be at liberty to say they are alive by that note. Instead try to think about what makes you you. This is often a difficult question to answer because you may never have asked yourself who you really are. But the answer is important because there in lies the key to your liberation. You may be thinking you are your memories, or the thoughts that others think about you.

Perhaps you think you are your dreams and aspirations, or worse yet, your body. These things, though they bear the appearance of value, are derivative of who you actually are. What if I told you that the nature of who you are is far more elusive than that?

Mental Projection

Mindfulness only starts to get at it but falls short of the experience itself. It Is only the doorway to who you are. Sit for a moment with your eyes open and just observe what's happening around you. Don't try to see this as a technique because it will pull you away from the present moment. Any form of analysis will separate you from the here and now. Just watch what's happening around you as you would a movie. Don't try to predict what will happen next or worry about if you're doing it right. Because, again, you'd be dividing your mind between past and future. Realize that there is no past and there is no future. Nothing exists but these fleeting seconds we call the present, the constant unfolding of now that never becomes then. Simply watch life. Don't judge it or give meaning to anything. Just watch.

Doing this long enough may give you a glimpse of what you truly are. You may realize as you sit there that you become the sounds around you, the things you feel and what you see. You will find that you become the observer and later after, with persistence, you'll become the experience itself. It won't take long either. Just sitting still and observing for a few minutes will result in this shift of awareness, which is exactly the point. Jonathan Kreiter, author of The Magnum Opus, talks about the power humans have to move their awareness beyond their physical bodies. To teach this he starts by explaining the spectrum of awareness and compares it to a radio.

If you were to close your eyes and imagine your favorite place to be, two things would happen. You'd begin to formulate the place from memory, molding it like sand, then you'd eventually see what you're imagining. It'd look dull and two dimensional at first but with enough practice you'd actually start to see the image clearly. This demonstrates an ability to move your awareness from one place to another. Consider this: you only remain in this reality, aware of the physical dimension we inhabit because of your five senses. You are constantly reinforcing your imagination of this reality. Science tells us our perceptions of reality are merely illusions produced by our brains.

If you're still having trouble believing you're more than the physical body you inhabit, think again about your dreams. If you're at all like me you've most likely had dreams where you were someone else. Ask yourself who you are in those dreams? Where are you while you're dreaming? Naturally you'd say you're lying in bed, but how then do you have an experience of another body. This is another sign of your ability to move beyond the body. This point is crucial to understanding the deeper mysteries of reality and harnessing the energies of the universe. enlightenment is more of a state of mind the more you begin to understand it. With what I've said in this chapter you should have an idea about the nature of reality and what it means to be enlightened.

Unlocking The Kingdom of Heaven

The present moment is the answer to the question of whether you are enlightened or not. The only difference between you and the guru you may look up to is location and patience. Sure, there is wisdom to gain from a teacher, but you have access to everything you need in the present. Take for instance the akashic records. If you were to do a google search for the term it would yield many results, all of which varying greatly in definition. Put simple, the akashic records is a collection of human experience, almost like spiritual genetic memory that we can all access. This can be thought of as the collective consciousness.

Now consider also that the present is the only thing that actually exists, which would mean the akashic records can only be accessed in this present moment. To further simplify this point, all knowledge must be available in this here and now moment and nowhere else. I wouldn't be surprised if that understanding doesn't sit well with you because it doesn't seem to leave room for the future or the eventual happenings to come. Where then does fate come in? Entertain, if you will, the multiverse and many world theories of quantum physics. It is entirely possible for there to be an infinite number of futures and be it that everything exists in this here and now moment, so would every conceivable reality. This gives you access to every possible future at any given moment.

The idea of the akashic record was first established in the ancient texts of the far east. Akashic comes for the Sanskrit word akasha meaning ether. The ether being a space beyond physical reality. When studied the akashic records in the contexts of the teachings of Jesus in the Gospel of Luke, specifically when Jesus is quoted as saying, "The kingdom of God is within you" (Luke 17:21), it become clear that Jesus was referring not just to the commonly held understanding of heaven, but also the collective consciousness of humanity. In many Hindu texts the akashic records are regarded as a divine place that can be likened to heaven. It's possible that Jesus wasn't just simply spreading platitudes but revealing the secret to taping into the hidden power of the universe.

All this to say, once you realize there is ever only the present moment and that the power to change your reality is and always has been within you, you can release yourself of the worry for the future and remove yourself from the torment of the past that binds you to imaginary worlds. Once your power is restored to you, you can go about crafting any reality you want. This is where manifestation truly happens. The moment you free yourself from the prison of your mind, you'll start to live the life of your dreams.

Chapter 4

You Shall Want for Nothing

In the game of life, you have to pick a character. It's not enough to take life as it is. You have to make a persona for yourself and thus pick a path to walk. Everyone has this path in mind and all it takes is the teaching of others and the rules of society to order your steps. I talked before about conformity and its power to rob you of a fulfilling life. This is sadly a taboo reserved for the entrepreneurs and lucky few among us to talk about. Many of us are perfectly content with working jobs that we don't like until we are too old to work it and then use those remaining years to do what we want. This is, more or less, a bargain that our society gives us in exchange for our freedom. It's a conditional slavery. The only difference between slavery and wage work is the idea that a wage worker will eventually not have to work. However, this is not the expectation. This society consumes people in the working class in the same way a lion consumes the antelope.

Like many others out there, I bought into the story that society tells us. That is, until I found the magic in the world. In order to free yourself from this tired narrative, you have to find the magic, or if you're lucky the magic will find you. In my case, the magic found me. This however didn't happen without effort. Where you do have to be found by the adventure, you have to be easy to find. It's best to look for the wonder in the world. I'm not saying that in order to be free from conformity you have to search for magic like I did. I'm saying you have to commit to figuring out who you are. When you do that the universe will start the game for you.

Now is a good time for me to address some common pitfalls along this road. Once you've set out to discover who you are, in whatever way that presents itself, you have to be ready to overcome the challenges that come along with it. In my case, pursuing magic, I ran into the challenge of power and being lost to it. Initially when someone here's not to let power control them, they may think it means you become obsessed by it. That's true but it's not the whole story. Power represents the opposite, which is the need that spawns it. I started my search looking for power because I felt weak and vulnerable.

Since I was young, I've had a strained relationship with my father, if you could actually call it that. My parental difficulties left me unsure of who I was and as a result I looked for approval from everywhere else, only to find further lack. The world showed me I wasn't valuable unless I was the best. The best at sports, the best in class, the best looking. Everything. I just knew that I had to be the best to get the love and approval I needed. This story is the same for everyone. If you take a moment and think about who you are and why you do what you do, and trace it back to its genesis, you'll likely find that you are looking for approval and acceptance from society. You, like me, are looking for worth even if it represents itself in a different way.

Luckily, I found the answers to my question of worth from spiritual uniqueness. Once I found a mentor that possessed the abilities I was looking for, I felt valued, different, but in a good way. For once in my life, I felt like I mattered. If you're reading this book, chances are you're looking for enlightenment to fulfill a lack in you of worth and acceptance. Perhaps you want to learn how to astral project so that you can leave the body and never return. If that's true, I know exactly how you feel. And I must be honest with you, that will not solve the problem. Why? Because the problem is required to help you grow. What you've asked for as a person, the dreams you have and the goals you've set to accomplish require you to be a specific type of person. That means you must endure the hardships because they will mold you into the right person for the job.

After learning how to astral project and the many extraordinary experiences that followed it, I found myself constantly hungry for more. It was a drug to seek and want and seek some more. It never ended. I went from experience to experience not satisfied until I thought I was, in some way or another, better than everyone else. It was the same insecurity that I had before I found the magic I was looking for. It didn't go away. It only got worse because I refused to address the source of the issue. On your pursuit for enlightenment, you will find yourself getting what you want and having it not fulfill you. Sometimes not at all. I remember living in a constant state of unfulfillment. I can't stress this enough, even that is a part of the process.

Part of the hero's journey is realizing you are powerful without the tool that made you a hero. Think about the marvel movie Thor Ragnarök. In that movie Thor's hammer Mjolnir is broken, leaving him powerless. Fortunately, at the end of the movie he realizes the hammer was just a tool to channel his power. He isn't the God of Hammers; he is the God of thunder. The same is true for us. The tools we use to find value in ourselves are not who we are. They are just the masks we wear to navigate through society and feel safe. All of that is created. We are more than who we think we are.

So why all the difficulty? Why not just change as you walk the path by getting what you're working for? I've found that the universe rarely allows you to be in a place you can't stay in. You must evolve to stay at the energetic level you wish to be at. We've talked a bit about the nature of manifestation and how it requires control over the mind. The same applies for the concept of enlightenment. All of this serves the purpose of getting you to the point where you realize you are the thing you are seeking.

Let's suppose then that Jesus knew this, if you cater tc this belief system. Let's say his way of convincing his followers of this fact was to let them experience the power for themselves. He would frequently say, ye of little faith whenever the disciples couldn't perform a miracle as he could. Jesus, as some would argue, came to demonstrate how a human can live in perfect connection with God. The kingdom of heaven is within you. This phase simply meaning you are the thing you are looking for. Hopefully I've drummed this point into your head enough by now. You are it. You are the destination.

I've spent so much time in my life looking for solutions to problems that don't even exist. You can find more of this philosophy in books like the open secret. It holds within its pages the idea that there is no one to have a problem, just as there is no problem at all. Life, as I've stated is a matter of hypnosis and we rarely ever even see life as it is. The simple method for undoing that self-hypnosis is to see the world without judgment.

Walking The Path

To help illustrate this point let me tell a story. Back some years ago my mentor and I were on a trip to downtown Chicago. We often took trips like this to visit a hole in the wall church gatherings. Well, I actually wouldn't call them church gatherings as they give the wrong idea. This sort of gathering didn't have the purpose of listening to a sermon or hearing about upcoming events as a normal church does. The attendants of this sort of gathering were a unique bunch who shared one thing in common; they were there to experience the presence of God. At the time this is all I knew to be right. Now, however, I understand the hunger these people had as a longing for enlightenment and the bliss of freedom.

Interestingly enough, the people who cultivated this presence, the energetic connection that the rest of the attendees longed for, often were the most sought after. I don't want to give the idea that enlightenment doesn't bring with it a certain presence. Someone who is living in connection with their truest self will have a powerful and liberating aura about them. Very interesting things happen when you encounter an individual in sync with who they truly are. Despite that, I often found myself chasing a feeling. Many people suffer from the same compulsion. Like me, others are chasing a high, a hysteria of emotion and feeling. It is of course a pleasurable thing to experience. But it isn't the point of the pursuit. To be technical there is no point but to experience, but it's impossible to do that when you expect everything to have a profound meaning beyond the enjoyment of the thing itself.

On this particular trip the group my mentor and I were visiting was conducting a 24-hour long worship event. This was a new thing for me to do. I had worshiped with my mentor before many times but very seldom with a group of people willing to worship 24 hour or until something happened. One would think if they called for heaven to come, they would eventually see an angel. That at least was my plan. My mentor had filled my head with such extraordinary stories that I could hardly contain my excitement. He however had been there and done that, so He didn't plan to stay the full duration. His loss, I thought. I planned to have my experience. No matter the cost.

To help better paint the picture of my expectations in this situation, let me share one of my mentor's experiences. Sometime after his conversion and spiritual maturity, after finally pursuing enlightenment of his own free will, he had an interesting encounter. Following a church service with a guest speaker who was especially peculiar, my mentor laid awake in the night feeling rather strange. Wind filled the room, and he began to feel a spinning sensation, as if he were on a merry go round. After a few minutes of this strange movement, he felt as though he was no longer in his room at all. He felt as if he was floating through space, in a void far beyond this physical world. This unbelievable feeling persisted until he felt dizziness overtake him, along with fear shortly after. In a moment, he felt his feet on cold concrete and saw a blurred image of a prison cell. Before he could catch his bearings, a man in the corner of the cell screamed, "You! It's you again!" This was one of the most terrifying experiences he had endured to date. Just before he was overcome with terror, he found himself placed comfortable back in bed.

It's stories like that that fueled my passion for the strange and peculiar. Up to this point I hadn't had my astral projection experience, nor had the angel appeared to me yet. I was virgin to the world of the mystic, yet I was totally sold on the life. It's important to note here before going on that if you assume you will need to venture far and wide to find the treasures of the present moment, you will have to do just that. I was in that position.

Once we had arrived at the gathering, I was pleasantly surprised to see that there were so many in attendance. The place was packed wall to wall with people reaching to the sky, singing, and kumbayaing. It was a very energetic environment. Not long after stepping through the door, a ram horn blasted behind me, standing my soul to attention and my heart to the brink of quitting. The assailant was revealed to be a nice old lady dressed as a Mardi gras hippy, bringing the good tiding of Christmas to a mall near you. She was as strangely dressed as one could conceivably be in such a gathering. However, her appearance gave off a sort of validity to the message she gave my mentor and I.

The strange old lady proceeded to give a prophetic word to us, telling us first about our drive to the event, who we were as people, and what we would do with our lives in the near future. I was dumbstruck, impressed, and honored at the same time. And for the record, if you find yourself giving a psychic reading, your goal should be getting a similar reaction out of your client, within the realm of truth. Don't sacrifice fact for flattery. The meeting didn't hitch for a moment after that strong opening. As we made our way through the crowded room, I noticed a group of people sitting cross legged in a circle. They looked to be withstanding hurricane level winds with the way they were swaying under some unseen power. I naturally was very curios.

At that moment, I noticed a man looking at me. Despite the normal social awkwardness accompanied by such a gaze, I felt like I knew him, as if I had met him before. I hadn't talked to him once, yet I knew we were friends. At the time I had no grid for such an auspicious feeling. Now, however, I would attribute it to reincarnation. After that encounter, we found seats and began to join the crowed of singing people, all of whom were trying to connect with something beyond themselves. Before too long the person I had seen in the group came over to me and introduced himself.

The first thing out of his mouth was a note about being sure we had met somewhere before. My newfound friend promptly invited me to join his group of very charismatic people. It didn't take long for me to feel right at home with them, totally swept up in the emotion and energy of the room. The session was very fulfilling to that part of me that needed the external validation of a unique group of people. I needed to feel like I was seeking with all my heart before I could accept the unconditional love that was always there. As I've said before, we are the gatekeepers of our own happiness. We live in cages and simultaneously hold the keys to our freedom.

My mentor eventually had his fill and suggested that we leave. The only problem with that was the fact I didn't feel like I had my experience. Even before I knew about enlightenment, I was searching for it. I wasn't satisfied with what I had seen and felt because it wasn't as grand as what I had been told about. Once again, I was creating the criteria for enlightenment to be valid. Because of this feeling in me, I told my mentor

I would drop him off at home and return, seeing as the event wouldn't end until the following day, and surely the ones who stayed the longest and gave completely of themselves would be most pleasing to God.

It turned out that returning was the right thing to do. When I got back to the event I was greeted by my new friend and his group, where they introduced me to the idea of visit another gathering of likeminded people and return to the event in the morning. That's when I realized none of these people knew each other. They had all met that day or a few days prior in like fashion as I had met them. They had been travelling all over the country from Redding California and had stopped here in Chicago as part of a bigger circuit. I was overjoyed to be a part of their group and gladly accepted their invite.

The Journey of Faith

My mentor had told me so much about his adventures and the spontaneity that brought them. His stories were always something out of a novel and I longed desperately for adventures of my own. So, naturally I had only one option; travel in the middle of the night with complete strangers looking for a church 2 hours away, hoping all the while that the pastor of that church would be waiting to open the doors for us. Oh, and did I mention the idea to travel to Wisconsin had come from a psychic vision one of the group members had, where they were shown the church and pastor. The vision showed the pastor waiting to let us in. Mind you, none of us had ever met the pastor or had attended that church.

I'm painfully aware of how silly such a faith-based trip was but at the time I was awestruck and for no other reason than to see if it was real, I wanted nothing more than to be a part of their weird little group. So, we began our trip. I can honestly say I wasn't afraid. I had so much faith in what I believed that I knew if we got lost, ran out of gas, or arrived at the church to find it closed, as it obviously would have been, something would happen in our favor. I was totally on board for it.

It didn't take long for us to get lost. After all, we had no real idea where this church was and we were going off the word of one of the women in the group, who could hear the spirit. It was all very loose and unorganized, but I didn't mind that. We found ourselves at a random Dunkin Donuts in a town we hadn't intended to visit. While there the old lady from earlier at the event sat with me, noticing my confusion and disbelief at the situation. I had faith but I was only human. We had driven around aimlessly for hours and had limited gas. It seemed like we would end up sleeping in the small jeep and bumming for gas money the next day.

She addressed my concern with patience. She told me this was one of many such adventures for her and that they always went something like this. Faith was the point. You may be wondering why someone who does magic and doesn't profess to be a Christian is talking in such depth about faith. The short answer is simpler than you might think. Faith is everything and without it you have nothing. Faith is what helps you push past your natural limits and do what you know is impossible. That faith doesn't have to been in a deity, it can be faith in yourself. Without faith, magic doesn't work. In the same way that you must feed the mind positivity to manifest the reality you want, you also must fill your heart with faith, the assurance that you have the power to create any outcome you want. You must believe you can make it happen.

Beth gave me a similar definition of faith. She said to me sometimes you have to take the leap. There will always be a situation where you must choose to do what you know or what you believe. Faith is trust, she told me. Now I realize that faith isn't just trust, it's trust in yourself. It's trust that the universe is conspiring for your good. It's trust that the story won't end before it begins. And most importantly, it's the trust that you matter, and that what you do, and who you are will impact the world. She ended by praying a prayer that has stuck with me to this day. She said, "Lord, let my ceiling be his floor." That's my prayer to you. I have experienced things that I even my mentor would be shocked by. And yet, I regard those things as merely the tip of the iceberg. It's my sincerest hope that my ceiling be your floor, that you transcend the established bounds of this reality. After all, that is the goal—to make leaders not followers.

Chapter 5

The Adventure of Life

I Lived a life of prayer in those days. I took Jesus at his word and prayed to be led. In prayer I learned the power of devotion and the vibration of love to open the doorway to heaven. I'll include the prayer and holy names I used to facilitate encounters with angels and divine appointments at the end of this chapter.

When Faith Pays Off

t was dark, the parking lot was empty, and we were in he middle of nowhere without food or water. If omething miraculous was going to happen, now was he time. I was noticeably anxious. The reality of the ituation was catching up to me. I didn't have money, ny car was back at the event building in Chicago, and I adn't eaten since earlier that day. This was the reatest test of faith I had ever been through. I could eel a similar anxiety coming off the other member of ur group. We were all waiting for a sign, a light on, or oor left open for us, anything. But there was nothing. t appeared we had driven through Wisconsin at 3 in he morning, stopped at the first church we found, and vasted gas for no good reason.

fter a long wait that felt like forever, Michael, my riend from the event, returned with his traveling artner. Their faces looked solemn, ready to present us vith the bad news. But out from the darkness behind hem came the pastor. I was speechless. The pastor shered us inside and gave us blankets and pillows to leep on. It was true. Everything that was seen in the ision was right. I had never been a part of such a tory. I had never seen the results with my own eyes. Iad I not sought the adventure, pressed into the fear, nd chosen to have faith in my desire to know more, I vould have never seen such a thing. The pastor had een waiting up all night for us to arrive because he too ad a vision that showed him a group of travelers oming to the church. He was even told the leader of he group's name was Michael.

The following morning the church service began, and t my surprise the congregation wasn't very large. There must have been no more than 12 people. I was so hungry for the experiences my mentor Dominic had told me about that I didn't care if there had only been 12 people in attendance. It was a drastic difference from how lively the event back in Chicago was. Nevertheless, the energy was potent. It felt just like it did in Chicago. The air was electric.

The Choice to Walk

The pastor began his sermon, which was coincidentall about faith, where he told his small congregation abou our miraculous trip. We had the typical time of prayer and worship then the interesting stuff happened. The pastor proceeded to give prophetic readings to the congregation as he felt led. He went from person to person giving inspirational words and insights into their future. Then he got to me. Apart from times with Dom, I hadn't gotten a prophetic word before.

He started talking about my character. And though he didn't know me, he was accurate as to the person I wa He told me I would be inspirational and that my reach and influence would change people's lives. He was ver specific as to how I would do that and gave me new adventures to look forward to. It was at that church that I learned about psychometry—the ability to touch an object and sense it's history. More on the strange psychic abilities one might experience along the road t enlightenment later.

Once the service was over and our group had returned to Chicago, we disbanded. They went off to their next scheduled location and I, having a normal life, returned home to tell Dom of my adventure. I was grateful to have met them but there was a bittersweet feeling when we parted ways. I still had the high from the trip we had taken but I also felt I was being left behind. I felt like I had gone on vacation in their interesting lives. I felt the same thing whenever I met someone new and had similar adventures with them. I found out that this feeling was the product of abandonment and a lack of self-worth. When you allow the adventure to be your identity, as soon as the adventure ends, you'll find yourself either searching for a new mountain to climb, or like me, you'll be lost. The adventure can only last forever when you realize you are the adventure. You are the path and the destination.

That pain of abandonment wasn't a new one for me. I felt it many times in my life and subsequently used it to determine my worth. The greatest of such pain came when my mentor left to start his life with his new family. He married a woman he had met while we were on a mission trip. We had spent several months together praying and seeking God, ministering to people in need, and developing as individuals. By the end of the trip, I had learned more in those few short months than I had up to that point. But like the adventure to Wisconsin, the adventure with my mentor had to come to an eventual end.

You Are The Path

It is true that when one door closes another one opens. In this case, one adventure has to end before another can begin. However, this transition can be painful, and people often get stuck in the fallout of them. It's easy to identify as the adventure, the search, or the goal itself. In order to avoid the pain of completion, you have to see yourself as the whole experience, the beginning, middle, and the end. Then you'll see that it's not the end of the book, it's just the end of a chapter of your life. You can be more than one character in this play of life as well. In fact, life is much more fun when you don't limit yourself to being a two-dimensional person.

It's interesting how you don't know your time with someone is nearing its end until it's over. The same can be said for a time in your life. It's so easy to believe a state of being will last forever. The harsh reality is that everything ends. It's impossible to accept the play of life without also accepting the end of that play. In the most extreme sense, death is the final scene of the play, the closing act. Unless you've found a way to cheat death, and trust me I'm looking, you will one day die. But before that day comes, you'll have a glimpse into the final act of other people's play. This is often seen as a tragedy, when it is perhaps one of the greatest moments to connect with someone.

The pain of loss isn't felt by the person leaving this world, it's felt by the ones left behind. And it is that same feeling of abandonment that I became accustomed to. In those moments of pain is an opportunity to experiences life. In those moments where the fun is over, the party has ended, and the people have left, when it's just you beside yourself, you can truly experience life. In those moments you are closer to God than you ever were during the adventure. In a way the adventure is just a necessary distraction.

The point of the adventure must then be to show you that you are greater than it. You overcame the challenge and beat the final boss. Both of which were created by you through perception. Every moment holds within it the bliss of the completed adventure. I'm sure you've felt that familiar twinge of pain when a trip is over, or when a friend leaves for a long time. That pain, though it is normal, comes from a place of incompleteness, from a feeling of loss. When you look back at the good old days and fantasies about how great things were, you are simultaneously missing how great things currently are. If you can recall, while you were in those moments you didn't see them as great nostalgia fuel.

The Prayer to Open Heaven

In the book of Isaiah in the bible, it is written, "Oh, that You would rend the heavens and come down, that the mountains would tremble before You!" (Isaiah 64:1). This plea echoes the ancient cries of those who sought a tangible connection with the Divine, yearning for the heavens to open and reveal the glory of God. Similar outcries to heaven are recorded in the Enuma Elish. These ancient tablets say the heavens were divided and the celestial realms established. The divine order was set, and through the power of the gods, communication between the realms was made possible

The following prayer acted as a primer needed to cleanse my spirit and awaken me to the energies around me. In using this prayer, you invite the universe to act on your behalf and open the door of divine encounters for you.

Great Spirit of the Universe, Source of all energy and life, I come before you with an open heart, seeking to connect with the infinite wisdom and love that permeates all existence. Just as it is said in the ancient texts, "Oh, that you would tear open the skies and come down," I ask that you remove the barriers between the earthly and the divine, allowing your light and guidance to flow freely.

These words are merely a template to illustrate the depth of emotion you should exude during your prayer and meditation time. I encourage you to make your own prayer and call to the universe for guidance. Feel your heart flowing with the energy of your request as you do, and the door to heaven will open for you.

The present moment holds within it the bliss of nostalgia. When you accept that every moment is special because you are there to perceive it, then the pain of abandonment or loss won't be pain at all. It'll be the start to your next adventure, the recreation of who you are. It'll be your invitation to explore more of yourself and your opportunities. But before you get there, before you can be reborn from the ashes of who you were, you must let go of who you are and embrace who you could be.

Chapter 6

Effortless Motion

So then, you find yourself face to face with the enemy. An army of obstacles present themselves, unmoved, intrepid, ready and armed to destroy you. You've finally accepted the call of the strange and unique, and now you must fight to defined what you believe. It isn't enough to resolve to uphold your new way of life, to chase fast after this dream of enlightenment, however illusory it is. The obstacles will come. After all, they must come. They must be there to challenge your resolve. To fully understand this view, or attempt to make sense of it, the necessity of evil or struggle in life, we must look further into Daoism.

To us in the west entertaining Daoist ideas is a difficult notion. To live in harmony with all, or the source, is a foreign concept. It initially requires the quieting of the self or the ego. We've talked extensively about the nature and ironic necessity of the ego, so I won't push too hard on it here. Suffice it to say, the ego is the antagonist in the pursuit of living in connection to the Tao. The core ideas held in Daoism assert that one should live in harmony with everything that exists. This idea is easier to accept when you believe you are a part of everything. You are something that the whole universe is doing, just as your cells are something that your whole body is doing, all be it unconsciously on your part.

The word Tao means "way" but can mean a number of things like doctrine or path. Its essence is the flow of the universe, the seamless transition of non-action to action. It is the epitome of effortless motion. Dao's belief revolves around the idea that all things are right as they are and to desire something is to pull it from a place of natural being. Dao is the art of acting without intent. or to put it more practically, it is the practice of living in the moment and letting your actions be natural and effortless, void of expectation.

You may see this as rather strange given our societal programing—work hard, climb the ladder, set long term goals, etc. All of these are great things to do and have merit in a capitalist society. However, when one looks to understand themselves and overcome the obstacles of doubt that lie before them, they must endeavor to move beyond the need to overcome. Again, this may sound strange at first but as I've said, sometimes to win you must stop playing all together. The same applies to life and the struggles that come with it.

Begin this herculean task of overcoming your challenges by first abandoning the notion of overcoming. To overcome means to overtake, conquer, beseech, take hold of something, you get the idea. These are phrases that don't make too much sense when you look at the challenges that will inevitable present themselves to you along your journey. Holding challenges and struggles in life at arms-length and believing they are separate from you is what perpetuates the problem.

I'm not saying it's impossible to grow or better yourself. Not at all. Where would self-help be if there was no hope of helping yourself. It is possible to evolve and heal from the wounds that made you, but the real question you should be asking is should you. Should you really undo the past trauma that acted as the chrysalis in your time of transformation. The natural reaction is yes. That's what this is all about right. We're here to learn and grow and develop. But have you ever asked yourself why? By the very fact that you are reading this book I know you've wondered what the meaning of life is. I'm sure you've come to the end of your rope plenty of times in life, following some self-help guru or money-making scheme, only to find yourself right back where you started.

The Play of Life

What then is the point to life? You may say, "Cal, that's obvious. The point to life is to be happy." If that's what you think, why then do you accept a life that won't bring you happiness. Let me be blunt. If you value money, you need money to be happy. Your sense of worth is attached to having and making money. If that's the case for you, I've got some bad news. That won't lead to happiness. If you don't believe me (and why should you? I'm not at all rich) look at the many wealthy people who have taken their lives. How, if money leads to ultimate happiness, have these people been so mentally troubled as to take their lives?

Surely, money doesn't buy or even ensure happiness. Why then do we dedicate our lives to it? Not only that, why do we chase after self-improvement if at the end of our lives we will all end the same. At birth we were all given a ticket. We all have a seat on the train that leads out of this life. No exceptions. Why then do we persist? Why do we fight against the tyrants in our minds and try to better ourselves? I would suggest you look inward for the answers. Why do you do what you do? What motivates you?

I say all of this to bring you to the point of no return in a way. I hope to help you see that the play of your life has acts, scenes of joy and pain, a beginning and an end, and that all of it is necessary. All of it is one. The moment you realize your life is a play, you'll start to watch it, to flow with it and accept where it goes. Happiness is less about what you've achieved, the lessons you've learned, how many people you've helped, or even how close to enlightenment you are, and more about enjoying the ride. When you watch a movie at the theater, you get invested. You may even forget you're watching a movie and begin to identify with the characters, feeling their pain, and basking in their victory.

Life serves the same purpose. You are watching life through the eyes of you character. You feel the good and the bad, the wins and losses, ups and downs. But just like a movie, it's all a part of the script. The good and the bad all come together to form the scenes of the movie you call your life. One cannot exist without the other. If the scenes of despair and emotional distress were removed from the story of your life, you wouldn't be who you are today. The story wouldn't progress. Am I saying life will always be hard and you'll always feel defeated? Of course not. That would be just as unbalanced as a story without challenges.

The play of life is one of balance. But often we don't see the balance. It's all too easy to see only the bad and overlook the good and visa versa. When you've been waiting for the good days to come, you find that the bad days multiply. This happens for a few reasons. First, you perpetuate suffering when you try to avoid it. When you push it away and long for better days, you create in that moment imbalance that the play of life must correct. In a way, you are getting exactly what you want. Your manifestation of 'happiness to come' is just that. Happiness to come, not happiness that has come.

Navigating Life's Hardships

At first glance this may sound impossible to fix. How can you not hope for change in a horrible situation? I know how you feel because I have felt the same. In the early days of my marriage, my wife and I lived in the basement of my family home, and we didn't have much money, if any at all to our names. We were two people with enough baggage to travel overseas for a year and still have bags left over. I was busy climbing the ladder of ambition, trying to give my wife and I a life of freedom, where we could enjoy our days apart from a perpetual work force. This of course kept me in and out of jobs and spending money on one business venture after the other.

I did everything from sales to making music and producing arts. I exhausted my creative resources trying to find an escape from the system. I tried many businesses like ecommerce stores, to coaching and social media marketing. I was just looking for a way out. I was looking for a life that didn't feel bound by destiny. One that didn't feel like the life of a peasant who would always struggle. Throughout that poverty and hardship, I didn't realize I was developing. I didn't see the joy and grace in the moment. It took many years but over time I discovered something more valuable than a business or stream of income. I discovered myself. In those years of struggle, I found my purpose, my drive.

The troubles of money didn't stop after I made that realization, but I was stronger. I had been refined by fire. And more importantly, I had a safety net to trust in the next time I needed to take a leap of faith. And the funny thing is every challenge that you face in life will be bigger and more frightening than the last. Every leap is higher than the one before. Life doesn't get easier as you go on. You just get more daring.

Any observation of life will show that nothing moves unless prompted to. Take the human body for instance. If left untended, the human body would atrophy and die. Pain and struggle are the fuel for growth. If the muscles in the body don't sense a need to grow, they won't. regarding nature, nothing would evolve without the need to. If life were perfect, devoid of danger and challenge, nothing would grow or evolve. It is challenge that causes us to thrive. But you must understand that to avoid imprisoning yourself in a worldview that prevents the natural flow.

You must accept the good along with the bad. But you know that. Why is that important here. The importance lies in the acceptance of challenge. What self-help and spiritual literature won't tell you is that you will fail. Even after you've succeeded. You must fail. You must come to the end of yourself to take off the old you like clothes so you can adorn yourself with a new outfit. We become stuck as people when we get comfortable in the identity that we currently have, afraid to accept the changes of life.

You are more than the identity you've developed. You are the hardships you've faced that have molded you. You are the dying, the pain, the struggle, and you are the hope, the joy, and the happiness in those very same moments. When you accept that you are the pain and the promise, you can see the moment as more than just the progression to a better time or a happiness to come, and you see the happiness as having arrived, even in the midst of you suffering. As I've said in previous chapters, if all things are here in the present moment, all things existing in the eternal now, then in any given moment there is joy and sadness. Enlightenment is also in that moment. It is the acceptance of all that is in that present moment, seeing all things as whole and complete. The journey, thought it be rot with trouble and danger, can be joy and happiness, even during the darkest times.

When you become comfortable in the dark, at peace with the shadows that form your contour, you'll be one step closer to realizing there is no *you* and there is no darkness. There is only oneness and the illusion of separation.

Part 2

Greater Mysteries of Inner Alchemy

Chapter 7

The Pillars of Magic

Having reached this far in the book, you should have a good grasp on the preliminary knowledge and understanding needed to begin the practice of magic. Though this book serves as the cure for the delusion and grandeur of enlightenment as people believe it today, the second goal of this book, one that requires the first, is to reveal to you the secrets that one is said to find once enlightenment has been attained. But seeing as we are all enlightened already, as I've been saying for many pages, we all have access to this knowledge that has been hidden for centuries.

Connecting The Current

don't mean that what I am to share with you in this econd half of the book is information that is impossible o find. What I mean to say is that this information has een misinterpreted, omitted, and outright withheld to reserve its uniqueness. There are groups on this earth hat seek to keep the masses blind to the powers and bilities that are their birthright. And to combat those hadow governments and organizations that seek to arvest our lifeforce, I have comprised the most owerful of the arts I have been taught.

The Illusion of Separation

Before you are able to dive headlong into such a pursuit f power, you must first understand that you exist in a ame as of right now. Consider, if you will, that this vorld is a simulation. There are many who believe this nd there is growing scientific evidence that supports his claim. Our society stands at the brink of a new era f technological advancement and integration thanks to he introduction of the metaverse and the spin offs it's ure to inspire. Graphics engines are now able to roduce graphics so realistic that distinguishing etween real and fake has become near impossible. A imple google search of unreal engine 5 will give you a irsthand example of the power we now possess to imulate reality.

Along with that there is augmented reality. This is a orm of technology that seamlessly integrates digital eality into our own reality once viewed through a hone or virtual reality headset. I mention these reakthroughs to illustrate that it is entirely possible hat we are living in a simulation of like sophistication.

Given that possibility, it is important to understand your place in this world.

Once you realize your freedom from purpose and reason, you can do what humans do best—add meaning and purpose to what we desire. So, what then are the essential pillars of magic? One must start with what I believe to be the greatest of endeavors: the understanding of self. You may scoff at this revelation, but its content is pure and efficacious. The self, as I've stated before, is the core of all things. You are not a member of the universe, hopelessly set adrift in this infinite sea of possibility, you are the sea only expressing itself as a cosmic wave, reflecting the very sea that it sprang from. You see, you are the code, the underlining fabric that fashions the universe you see. It's already understood that we are the stuff stars are made of. We are that which persists all around, divided only by word and judgments.

This concept of oneness with all things must be understood fully in order for you to have the faith within yourself to persist when reality does what it does best, rise up against you. You must know you are the challenge as well as the challenger. There is no separation. This is the first and most important pillar, from which all others find support. From this understanding comes the expression of control, or manipulation of the reality that you now see as yourself. Don't try to bend the spoon. Any pursuit after the etheric apart from an understanding that the etheric is you unbound is futile.

There are several types of expression of the control I speak of. The first and most readily known is manifestation and the law of attraction. The list that will follow in this chapter about the methods to use manifestation will not be exhaustive simply because there are hundreds of techniques one can find. What's more important is the principle behind the power, what makes it work. Like any source of power, there are ingredients to its production. And I assure you, every type of manifestation and act of will on reality relies upon these key ingredients.

The Power of Will

The first of these is will itself. All too often do aspirants of this art of magic begin their pursuits without a clear end goal. You must know what you want before you begin any working, ritual, or spell of any kind. Your will guides the power that will flow as a result. Will is the capsule that consciousness inhabits. It is not the brain that holds consciousness, you see, because it is will that persists long beyond the body. It may appear to be naturalistic when someone leaves a will behind, but if you look deeper, you'll find the hidden truth. Beyond power is will, and within will is consciousness.

The disciples of Christ were taught to pray by first saying,

" Our Father, who art in heaven,

hallowed be thy name,

thy kingdom come,

thy will be done,

on earth as it is in heaven.

Give us this day our daily bread.

And forgive us our debts,

as we forgive our debtors.

And lead us not into temptation,

but deliver us from evil.

For thine is the kingdom,

and the power, and the glory,

forever. Amen."

When one studies the life of Jesus as presented in the gospels, they find that Jesus leaves clues as to how one might live as he did. I've said before in this book that Jesus was an example as to how we can operate in this world. One of those clues was will. To further illustrate the power of will and its necessity, you can look at its origin. Jesus draws his assurance from God the father. By saying thy will be done, he is in effect invoking the authority of God. To arrive in a foreign land and say you come in the name of the king to fulfill his will, is to make that new land liken unto the king's land. It is a display of your power to invoke such will.

Using your will, spirits will take what you've asked and transform reality to look as you will. Now there are many rules to the expression of will. To use it properly you must be able to hold your mind and emotions captive. They betray your will if left unchecked. They rob from you the very aim of your working. I speak now about magic and the manipulation of reality to your desires. You must master first the mind and all its faculties. This task alone is one that can take lifetimes. Fortunately for us, there are methods that speed up the process of mental control. Your will is what makes you an individual, your freedom to choose how you live and what that living produces.

Understand that your will shapes your reality. This is vital to know before we move forward. It should be known now that you, the reader of this book, Are God incarnate. With that position comes tremendous responsibility. You see, if you are the fabric and lining of the universe, that can only mean that this world is a product of your own design. It is you that has made the world this way. All that you perceive around you, it's expression and nature, was in direct result of your will for it to be so. Take time now to think about all the events in your life and understand that it is you who control them. Find the invisible strings that connect the hearts and minds of the world back to you.

The Yogic Tradition of Will

You may be wondering what you do with this knowledge. If the world really is subject to your will, what must be done? You must take control of your mind. Take control of your fear, your hatred, and your self-loathing. Living the life of a magician is not an easy path. It is a path where you accept the results of your actions and feel the weight of the world you've created. You are creating the very world you live in from one moment to the next. Thinking isn't enough when it comes to this level of control. Will is not confined to thought alone. Will is all encompassing. It is the embodiment of focus and concentration.

The yogic traditions of the far east suggest that it is through mental tranquility maturing into deep concentration that leads to union with source or enlightenment. Nearly all of will is wrapped up in the brain and your ability to control and direct your attention for extended periods of time. That isn't all. Once your mind is properly trained to be calm and focused, you must then let it go once again and ride atop your mind as it guides you to the desired goal, the aim of your will. Therefore, your will, what you desire, should be all encompassing. It should be who you are inside and out. This is done simply by devoting yourself to reflecting in yourself the image of what you want. This is why people say to change the world you must first change yourself.

The Magic of Mental Mastery

Now comes the subject of your practice. I assure you that all you learn and practice pertaining to the development of your mental mastery will be directly used in the later stages of magic and mysticism. Abilities like astral projection, second sight and connection with spirits requires your focus to be of adequate standing. Will can be broken down into three parts. Once all three parts have been mastered, or at the very least explored, you will find access to magic comes easy as there will be no hinderances.

There are many ways of going about this feat of mental mastery, but it is best to present the formula from which all meditation techniques come. I mean to make you a master of many arts. To do so I must present to you the simple ingredients that once combined form the desired outcome. In yogic tradition there are three stages of meditation. All other practices with the aim of controlling the mind and connecting back to source, rely on these three stages. Even hypnosis and trance state, once broken down resemble this simple three step process.

Pay attention first to the mind apart from intervention. As stated before, you waste your energy regretting the past and fearing the future. The normal human thinks about many different things throughout the day. All of which are normal and natural to think about because they pertain to your survival. This is useful in the busy beta brainwave society we operate in. When you seek to work with realms beyond the physical, operating as others do is useless. This goal of mental mastery not only brings you to a very real sense of enlightenment, it also pulls your power back to you so that you are able to do magic when you are ready. Often when an aspirant attempts to work a spell or astral project, they simply lack the spiritual power to do so.

The first of the three stages is the easiest to get into naturally, and can be done anywhere. it is represented by the Sanskrit symbol धरणा and translates to Dharana the sixth limb of yoga. For those of you who like to have a full peripheral understanding of all the practices I refer to in this text, you'll find more about the foundations of yoga by searching for the 8 limbs of yoga. The final three limbs pertain to meditation, which is our primary focus. The preceding five limbs have to do with a healthy mind and body, all of which can be achieved through any number of physical exercises and diet.

Focusing the Mind

Dharana can best be described as holding or maintaining attention on a fixed object. The essence of dharana is to restrain one's mind as one does a horse or dog. The mind is very much the stallion of our being as it is ready at any moment to run off with any idea it sees as the shiniest. To put it simply, dharana is the practice of holding your attention on one fixed object for a prolonged period of time without distraction. It's the practice of making your mind a dot. You can use any object to narrow your focus. For my clients I have them draw a dot on a piece of paper and tap it to their wall. I then instruct them to look at that dot for five minutes.

During this exercise many people find they cannot stay focused for more than a few seconds. The more experienced meditators will last a bit longer, but the normal untrained person is lucky to focus for a full minute. The mind is just too loose and uncontrolled in the beginning. What you'll notice during this exercise is that you will suddenly find yourself somewhere else, no longer sitting in front of the wall staring at the dot. You'll be off in a memory somewhere or focusing on some task you must complete that day. It is far easier than you think to move away from this reality and start to experience another. One of the many lies I seek to uproot is the idea that you are trapped in your body, a slave to your flesh. This notion that astral projection is a difficult process is what stops you from achieving it. As I stated, you are creating your reality along with the challenges you face from day to day.

To practice the development of dharana, spend some time focusing on an object. It is easiest to start with something that's alive. In most case that's a plant or even a rock. Find an object to put your attention on. Many of my clients like staring at a candle flame. When you do so focus on the fine edge of the fire, the aura of the flame's body. It seems to be easy to hold your attention on something when it's detailed. You'll want to conduct your practice in a quiet place free from distraction.

The mind is only limited by the perception of limitation. With a practice like this a common pitfall is believing you are unskilled. This is untrue. I've said you are unskilled because you may lack confidence. What you must understand is that you have been taming your mind for years. Every time you daydream you are allowing the mind to ride free of your control, to do whatever it pleases. The same power that is exerted to transport you from this world to another via astral projection is the very same power you must hold in this here and now moment.

Once you've given some days, if not weeks to this practice (This shouldn't be rushed. This game of enlightenment and magic is a marathon) you should be comfortable calming and quieting your mind. Once you're able to do this you can have a bit of fun exploring your inner universe. To do this, simply sit in a comfortable place and begin to focus on your breathing, or any external object. Placing your attention on internal things such as the heartbeat and the breath serves to pull your awareness from your surroundings. This helps to prepare you for the next stage of meditation.

If you persist in this holding of your attention on one object you will experience a shift of consciousness. This is a light trance. Your brainwaves are slowing from beta frequencies to the more relaxed and introspective alpha frequencies. Spending time in this state will familiarize you with how your consciousness moves beyond the body. This is useful for placing your energy into objects and perceiving the thoughts of others. I'll talk more about this later.

The Results of Focused Awareness

I've had a number of exciting experiences doing this practice. One such occasion was during my time as a camp counselor. The summer days were long and hot, and the children were harsh weights on my mind. It was at that time I decided I wouldn't be working with kids anymore for a very long time. I was in way over my head with that job and by the end of the summer I was feeling how tired I really was. One night after returning to my cabin I decided to spend some time meditating. The lack of free time had put a damper on my energy.

With a moment of free time to spare, given that it was very late, I was able to settle in and meditate. Once the basics of energy work are mastered, true joy and relief comes from it. This night I laid in bed and simply watched my energy flow. A technique I teach my clients is one I like to call the observation of what is. It's a pretentious name for a rather simple exercise. All one must do is sit and observe whatever is happening in the body. At first there may be nothing. But given time and patients, one will start to feel the movements of their energy body.

While doing that exercise, I noticed the energy sensations beginning to build. At this point in my journey, I hadn't felt so much energy before nor did I have as much control over it as I did in that moment. I know now that you don't control the energy, you are the energy. It is you. Realize then that you do not bend the world to your will. Rather, you are the world bending. It was at that point the energy within me began to move on its own, and I truly was just observing it. It had a mind of its own. Like lapping waves on the beach, the currents of electric energy washed over me, ebbing and flowing in and through my body.

There came a moment during this cascade of cosmic force where I began to lose my surroundings. Not as one does while drifting to sleep, but the way you do when you first wake up. It was a feeling of no longer being restrained. Out of curiosity I opened my eyes just in time to see the ceiling above disappear, burning away from the corners of my vision like paper lit from the edges. In seconds the scene of my cabin was replaced by an empty field of vibrant green, backed by a bright yellow sky. Wherever I had found myself the sun was setting, and I was alone.

The transition was seamless. So much so, that I could hardly believe I wasn't still laying on my bed in that old cabin. I studied my surroundings and was amazed at the pulsating colors. Everything was alive and breathing. And there was this overwhelming scene that I was the environment I found myself in. It was as if I could feel my breath in tandem with the world around me. Before I knew it, I was lying in bed again, the heavenly image having melted away like morning fog from my eyes. I laid for a long while just basking in the flow of the persistent energy that lingered.

Chapter 8

Going Beyond The Body

Reality breathes in time with you when you slow yourself to notice. It is true that all of life is a play unfolding, that once noticed commences with its acts. You can go on living your life without ever taking time to notice the play of life unfolding before you, and only for you. In any given moment there is a symphony of grandeur awaiting your slightest gaze, longing all the while to be seen. For the one simple reason that it can be perceived. Within ever moment of time, the here and the now, the only thing that exists is you, the perceiver. Because it is when you perceive the world around you that it exists.

Having now examined your awareness you should be well ready to proceed. I know there are many who will read through the entirety of this book without having taken the time to do any of the exercises suggested. This is a disservice done to yourself. Everything I present should be tested if for no other reason than to determine its worth. Take nothing I say as absolute without first discerning for yourself what you make of it. The same goes for the pillars of magic. You may choose to take this information and do things in a totally different way than I have suggested. The only important things to take away from this are the tools I'm presenting to you. Simply add them to the already full box of methods and techniques you don't use.

That said, the next stage of meditation one will undoubtedly experience with persistence is referred to as Dhyana. The Sanskrit symbol ध्यान translates to Meditation in English. This, however, isn't the full weight of the word. Dhyana can mean concentration, reflection, and profound states of connection. Dhyana occurs when one's attention is placed on an object for long enough to still the mind to one pointedness. Once the mind is quieted, one begins to associate themselves with the object of meditation. This can be a thought or object.

The result of such deep meditation is the connection between the object and the mediator. You will begin to gain gnosis about your true self, the nature of who you are and the fullness of your life. It's a rather strange concept to think you can simply stare at a leaf and begin to know yourself and subsequently the universe.

But, my dear friend, that is the reward of the present moment.

Transferring The Mind

The followers of yogic tradition have used this method, along with Dharana, to draw themselves closer to source. It is a funny thing to pursue enlightenment. Because you must search to find that you need not have searched at all. Practices like this are a gentle way of guiding oneself to the shore of this great understanding. How then is this possible? Why does it work? To surrender yourself to a practice of this kind is to willingly put yourself through torture. This method is one that takes time to see progress in. The reason for that is because there is no progress to gain.

The point of this practice is firstly to strengthen your will, and secondly to reveal to you that once your will is strengthened you can willingly let it go. Again, this matter of enlightenment is a paradoxical one. You must gain control to realize you don't need to have control in the first place. So then, to proceed, simply rest your attention on an object. This method resembles, and in all likelihood was the origin, of a technique called psychometry. This is an ability to understand an object, its history, and energetic signature, by simply touching it or directing your attention to it.

The effect of dhyana is to receive information from the object you are observing. You'll find that you are the object and the information gathered is about another facet of yourself. When I focused my attention on this practice, I started with plants. Before long I could place a portion of my awareness into the plant, like an astral arm. I would mentally imagine myself as the object, seeing from its perspective, feeling what it might feel. Often, if given enough effort, I would begin to feel reality from the object. Much like the exercise I gave earlier in this book. The purpose of that exercise is to help you move your awareness.

Expanding The Mind

An extreme example of this connection can be seen when one takes psychedelics. Beyond the physical effects of the substance lies the spiritual effect one has. The sense that they are connected to everything is usually reported. This is because the boundaries between self and object dissolve when the mind is quieted. Psychedelics do a good job at keeping us in the moment, for obvious reasons. This effect, however, can be achieved with the given meditation technique. When you focus on an object for long enough, apart from judgment about that object or your skills to observe it, you'll find that you identify with the object.

This concept of learning or gaining knowledge of oneself from the observed object may sound strange, but it should be rather easy to understand. If you start from the basis that you are everything, then place your awareness, the only thing keeping you present in this body, into the object of your focus, you will, in some part, become that object.

As with many of my experiences in this land of mysticism, they began with substances. In this case cannabis was the vehicle of my ascension. I've had many strange voyages with the substance and have established a working relationship with it. Meaning I treat it as a coworker. I respect its ability to distort and liberate the mind. One rather strange occasion I found myself becoming the people around me, the objects and the environment. This as anyone would suspect was jarring.

It was a normal family outing, my girlfriend, her brother and his wife, a few friends and myself. After some peer pressure to smoke, and an accidental consumption of much more than was intended, I found myself far more faded than what was comfortable. These experiences usually follow some period of physical discomfort. The group was to set off for six flags, an hour-long trip. By the time we took off I was about ready to vomit. I had felt the effects before, and I could usually handle myself after having done too much. But this time I was lost at sea and there was no land in sight.

Before my eyes I began to see the road before us tilt as if it were being lifted from one side. I thought for sure that I'd fall right out of the car window and float away. Time passed achingly slow and sound along with it, the sound of car engines stretching in the distance. as I often do, I prayed for the experience to stop. But it didn't relent. In time I submit to the substance and accepted what I felt and saw of the now orange tinted world around me. This acceptance came with a release of fear and effort. After a short while I began to relax and almost sink into myself.

That's where I began to see it. I started to see a tunnel behind my closed eyes. It was a boxed tunnel that banked and shifted in the darkness of my eyelids. I could see it clear as day. I had never seen anything like it. Along with what I saw came the feeling of inertia. I wasn't just sitting in a car; I was flying effortlessly through a blue tunnel. I traveled the length of the tunnel until I reached its end and arrived in space. In that void of space, I saw different scenes playing out. There was the image of a beach to my left and another of a school to my right, floating there in the void.

It was just then that I remembered my place in the car, who I was and where I was going. More importantly, that I wasn't alone. I began to think about the people in the car with me. At first my thoughts rest on their words, then, with my eyes still closed, I began to see them, like silhouettes in the dark. As I persisted in my focus, I started to feel my wife next to me. But not as though I was touching her but as if I was her. I could feel her weight shift in the seat, the heat on her body, and the restriction of the clothes she wore.

With this new perception came the strange perception of myself, or what I understood to be me, as a ball of light, wisping from one person to the next. In that car I became everyone. I felt their emotions and could perceive their thoughts. It wasn't an impressive feat at the time because for a moment I understood that I had woken up to the truth. I was the only one in the car.

Experiences like that aren't uncommon for people when they focus their mind on a single object. To pull your awareness from the scattered themes that entertain it to a single point is to gather your spiritual power back to you. Following this connection with reality you'll experience while practice this taming of the mind, you'll move on to the final stage of meditation. And although we have talked in great length about connection being a state of being rather than an object, it is very much both. But you can't act out of a place of lack.

The Paradox of Power

That is the great paradox of life. You must have what you seek before you receive it. To grab hold of the illusory you too much be illusive. You must discover that you possess what it is you want, or at the very least believe that you ought to have it. Enlightenment is perhaps the most elusive of states to achieve. It is a delicate balance between holding and letting go. This meditation technique is the training one needs to learn to left go while holding on tight.

This concept was expressly taught to me by my mentor. He would say you must let go of control to truly have it. Then you'll see you don't actually need it. The importance of will power is realizing the two halves—will and power, are one whole. The goal of yoga is to become one with God. It is union. These steps you take as you move through life are all meant to draw you closer to an understanding that there is only oneness, the masquerade of many and the actuality of one. You find that the product is also the producer, the painting is the essence of the painter.

The knowledge of self that one gains during dhyana is deeper than logic and reason. It is a knowing. It is a calling back to who you are; it's not a struggle or a striving, just as there is no struggle to wonder from where you came. The purpose of two is to discover there is one. Through this practice, I hope you will find that all other states of reality come naturally. After all, the only thing being done with all this mediation, is a silencing of the judge in our minds so that we see clearly the reflection in the mirror.

Chapter 9

Encountering Source Consciousness

Though I've spoken at length about the naturalistic side of connection, there very much persists something extraordinary about the experience of it. It takes one first to realize that it is a falsehood to imagine that enlightenment is somewhere else. There is greatness to behold in the moment and moments of your rapture in cosmic ecstasy. I've heard many such stories from practitioners and skeptics alike. They spoke about lifting out of their bodies and being transported to a place beyond time. Some say they met God, and others say they were God in some way. But the stories all have one thing in common, they involve something quite extraordinary.

To believe enlightenment is a onetime experience is to dilute its effect when it does happen to you. You'll find yourself living from one experience long ago, and to some this is acceptable. But why live off old memories when you can forge from the same fire new ones. To be alive is to explore and evolve and change. After all, you must change. Nothing that exists within time is immune to its effects. Be it that you must every day become something greater or more refined than the day prior, it only makes sense that enlightenment would be a book of experiences. Better yet, enlightenment is a lifestyle of awakening.

Connection to source consciousness and the magic that inevitably springs from it is a lifestyle. Due to our power over our own realities, it is entirely possible that, if left untended, your life would fall out of balance. As I said in the previous chapters, life is a balancing act of holding and letting go, acceptance and rejection. Enlightenment works in the same way. The razor's edge between life and death is such that if your desire wavers, or you express a variance in your beliefs about the world you are fashioning, there will be chaos. It is vital then for you to hold one thing in mind, to be singular in your pursuits.

The Key to Angelic Visitation

The pillars of magic that I've observed show that one must know themselves, have a strong sense of will and mental toughness to endure the challenges that will no doubt arise, and possess within themselves the power. The last of the three pillars deals with the outward display of magic, the manipulation of reality. Like many areas of study pertaining to the mind and its control over perception, one must first calm the storm within the mind before they can quiet the storm that rages around them.

By this point you should understand that the universe is a mirror that reflects the thoughts you cast into it. You wouldn't look into a mirror, and upon seeing a blemish, wipe the mirror. You, being a person of sound mind, would know the mirror only reflects what it is shown. The power of the mind is so great that it will cast on the world your inner thoughts and reshape your external environment. Most of us cast horrific thoughts onto the world and try then to wipe away the mirror to change things. I continue to harp on this point because it is the foundation of everything I am talking about in this book. You are so powerful that if you simply believe you are already enlightened and that your life is beautiful, then reality will reflect that.

This is what one will experience once they reach samadhi, the final stage of meditation. Represented by the Sanskrit symbol समाधी, samadhi can be described as one having reached a level of connection or oneness with the object of their focus, whether it be a deity or a normal object. After having quieted the mind and identified yourself with the object of your attention, it is said that one will gain a super consciousness or awareness of the true self. Some also describe this experience as feeling like you've suddenly moved away from the body.

The draw back to such an experience is that it is difficult to achieve. In most cases such an experience of oneness with source is an accidental one. But I must stress that it's not a one and done experience. You don't reach the mountain top of meditation and float away from life. Not until you're dead, that is.

In Sean Webb's book 'Mind Hacking Happiness volume 2' he talks about his experience of non-localized awareness. During his retelling of events, he mentions that it was a total accident. He details his process of learning to quiet his mind, as we talked about in the previous chapter, and the difficulty he faced in doing so. If you've spent any time trying to silence your monkey brain, you'll know just how difficult of a task it is. People new to the art of meditation mistake this as stopping all activity going on in the brain. This just isn't possible. Pictures and abstract sound will persist while you try to quite your mind. In fact, pictures and sounds will increase as your brain wave frequency begins to slow. It's a natural process of trance induction.

What Sean describes is learning to stop the subvocalization happening in the brain. You do that by focusing on internal bodily processes like the heartbeat and the breath. Not only does that pull your energy back to you but it also helps to connect you with your subconscious mind. This happens because you're reducing the many thoughts in your head and thus clearing the fog that's preventing you from making connection with the other parts of yourself. He goes on to say that after a few weeks of dedicated practice, he got comfortable taming his mind. But nothing ever really happened. Until he spoke to God or the universe or whatever he thought was out there. He said, "if you want me to know more, I'm in." and that was it. He laid back on his bed and quieted his mind. Before he knew it, he was feeling overwhelming surges of energy rushing through him. And like the fear I felt during my first astral projection experience, he thought he was going to die.

In an instant he was pulled up and out of his body and appeared in space, where he met God. If you'd like to hear the rest of his account, I encourage you to get his book. I mentioned that story to illustrate just how random and unplanned his experience of enlightenment was. I believe there are two reasons for this difficulty. Firstly, the problem may lie in our idea of what enlightenment is and the work we must do to obtain it. We begin the journey believing it is a godly, out of reach experience that only the monks on the mountain get to have. Thus, we manifest that type of reality. Second, we must be in some way inhibiting the experience by practicing these techniques. I believe we cloud the sky. We somehow block what is already happening all around us.

Connecting With The Inner God

It is entirely possible that we all are connected to God at every moment, floating through the infinite expanse of space, one with all forms of life. But we don't see. Every story I've heard of enlightenment experiences has had that key factor in common; it was an accident. Though the practitioner may have been seeking it, the breakthrough happened apart from their effort. And sure enough, enlightenment happens to people who aren't looking for it at all. People who have no religion or belief in a higher power at all.

It must then mean that no amount of effort will get you to that goal. And since I've written this book with the goal of baring to you the truth, I must say again, you won't ever attain enlightenment. That is the cure for the sickness of longing and seeking for it. Realize now that it is not something to be obtained or acquired. How would you hold it? In what way would you wear enlightenment? How would you show off a state of being that reveals there is no state of being?

In the book Autobiography Of A Yogi, Paramahansa Yogananda talks about many esoteric experiences. One of which was the day his mentor showed him divine consciousness firsthand. His account of the story was miraculous. He describes one day being called away from his meditations by his mentor. At that time his meditations were little more than exercise of quieting the mind. He had never had a transcendental encounter, until that day. His mentor laid a hand on his chest, and right then he could see everything around him; he could even see clearly through walls. He could see energy and could feel the divine Om.

Such experiences are fascinating but require the intervention of an outside source. In this case it was the yogi's mentor who initiated it. Many of my experiences, though they don't happen often, have occurred by happenstance. It is possible to set your life up in such a way that you increase the odds of having these kinds of encounters. As I said, enlightenment is a lifestyle. Which means that when you are living your normal everyday life, you are still mindful of the present moment, still aware of your divine connection to all things. Living in such a way is the best advice I can give to experience spontaneous enlightenment.

Encountering The Guardian Angel

Many years ago, I had one of my first encounters with, what one would call, divinities. At the time I had only heard about angels and their influence, but I had never seen or heard them. My mentor filled my head with stories about his adventures with spirits all the time. I was ready for my own encounter. But like enlightenment, it happened apart from my control. At least apart from my control in the way society understands it.

Prior to the event I had been spending a great deal of my time meditating and seeking God. Such is the recipe for these things. Just keeping your porch light on is all you can do. If encounters want to visit, they will. Somethings are divine timing, but others have to do with your openness. In my case, I had been praying for such an encounter for years. One night my prayer was answered. After hours of prayer and worship I went to bed only to have an auspicious dream about a friend. I awoke to the sound of talking.

At that time, I slept on a couch with family. The room I was in had a couch with a love seat on the opposite side, divided by a small, glass coffee table. At around 3 in the morning, I awoke to the sound of talking in the room. I quickly realized there was someone pacing back and forth on the other side of the coffee table. The being's appearance was that of stars sparkling in the night. I couldn't see its features apart from the shimmers and glints of light that outlined it. The air around it seemed to buzz as it paced. As it moved through the room it was saying, "Our bodies are temples for the living God. We must be holy as he is holy."

When the entity noticed I was awake it looked over to me and said, "you are a son." When it spoke the word son, it appeared before me on the couch and slammed its hands down on me. The power I felt was unbearable. It felt like lightening was shooting through my body. The entity went on to say, "You will run to heaven." When it finished, it disappeared, and I began to scream as the currents of energy blasting through me caused me to levitate up and away from the couch. I continued up to the ceiling and hovered there about a foot away.

Softly and slowly, I descended to my original position on the couch. The room was dark once again, the glowing Specter having vanished. I laid there until the sun shone through the curtains, sweat soaking my clothes. For several days following that encounter I would wake to find a glowing being sitting beside me. Events like this happen rarely, but when they do, they impart faith and courage to persist in your pursuit. It is my hope that using the techniques in this book you too have these transcendental encounters, as it is your birth right. Miraculous things are happening around you even now as you read. It is only because the fog around you is so thick that you don't see and experience.

Connecting The Current

Enlightenment is always happening because that is all there is. It is through the use of our powerful minds that we create these smokescreens that block out the rays of samadhi. It is imperative then that you commit yourself to learning who you are, gaining control of your will, and mastering the great power that resides within you.

Chapter 10

The Pillar of Power

Power is of particular importance in the reality. With it we've marched on past the limits of evolution and forged for ourselves a world of comfort and prosperity. With power, weapons are built, battles are fought, and wars are won. It is with power that all things are done. I'm speaking now in the physical sense. You know now that all things are energy. The only thing stopping you from passing through a wall is the vibration of the molecules in your body and that of the wall being too slow. What then of power and energy? Why are they important. Since all is done with the use of energy, it is vital that you learn to regain your lost energy and focus from the struggles of the world that took them from you.

Connecting The Current

We've talked already about the first two pillars of magic. Now I'll explain the final pillar. Once all three are mastered, or at least understood, one will experience enlightenment and the fruits there in. The pillar of power can be the most confusing to learn. There are plenty of sources out there that claim to give you abilities and have the definite route to true arcane knowledge. I can assure you that there is no such infallible source on this material. All that has been amassed are techniques that have proven beneficial for others to achieve enlightenment and awaken their psychic abilities. Let me be clear, you will have to experiment with many such techniques before you find one that works for you.

Therefore, I plan to give you the basic building blocks and formulas you need to create your own process to gather energy and awaken your psychic abilities. Since we've talked about the theory quite a bit, it's time to dive into the technique more heavily. This pillar deals with the accumulation of energy from various means. All to the effect of reaching enlightenment and awakening your natural psychic abilities. The first things we will focus on are connecting with the subconscious mind, the seat of inner psychic power, and the development of the energy body. Every good psychic development system should focus on two primary goals, changing one's beliefs system, and becoming familiar with the feel and flow of energy.

Reprogramming The Mind

Most people walk through life under a self-induced hypnotic trance. They talk themselves into circles about who they are and what power they have in life. They convince themselves they are slaves to life, unable to change who they are. This is the first place to start if you are to reach lasting enlightenment and bear the fruit of such a state. One must first break the illusion of imprisonment before they can live free, even if there is no cage that holds them. The greatest cage of all being the human body and false belief that comes with it: “All I am is this flesh and blood.” By now you should understand you are more than just your body. But there are other beliefs that shape who you are that are getting in the way of your natural psychic abilities. You remember when I said enlightenment is all there is and that it’s happening all around you? Well part of that happening is your innate ability to transform the world around you, and to tap into your psychic abilities.

To begin with are practice on this pillar, start by finding out what it is you believe about the world around you, the people you encounter, the things that transpire. Really figure out what you believe. One exercise I teach tells students to follow their beliefs and trace them back to the source. What caused that belief to surface? Find out what the origin of your beliefs are. A rather effective way to go about this is to simply ask yourself why after you discover a core belief. For instance, you may think life is hard and that you must work hard to be happy. If that is a belief you hold, you would then trace that belief back to its origin by asking why you think that’s true.

This practice of simply asking yourself why will often lead you to memories, sometimes traumatic ones. Before we progress, I should tell you that any system that seeks to bring you closer to God, as it were, will inevitably result in you addressing your past and current traumas. Who you are has been shaped by the people around you, by what they said and did pertaining to you. You've learned to treat yourself as they did, to see the world as they did, and finally to limit yourself based on what they thought was possible. This is why you must change your belief system. Really find out what you think about life and why. Often times you'll realize you don't actually believe what the world has been telling you. Power is first in the mind. Therefore, you must start by liberating the mind from its mental shackles.

To begin the intense mental cleaning work, you should start by writing down your beliefs. Write down the facts about yourself and the world that you believe are hindering you from getting closer to source. It may take you some time to come up with this list and the list may be quite long. This is fine. The goal here is to identify your limitations so they can later be broken. You must first find the boundary lines before you can cross them. You'll have to explore yourself.

Mental Framing

If you still find it difficult to figure out what you believe in you can try this mental framing exercise. This exercise will reveal to you how you think and feel about certain topics. Start by writing in your journal from the perspective of an alien who has visited earth. On this visit make note of everything you experience. You can pretend as much as you want here. Write about what you see humans do, how they act and respond to the environment. Make note of your thoughts about food and health, and how you perceive humans to feel about this. If you want to really be out there, pretend you're and alien from another dimension that doesn't understand why humans eat at all. Make observations about governments and cultures. Talk about how people treat you. Do you reveal yourself secretly to higher up members of government, or do you interact with the common folks?

I've found that I come up with some very interesting perspectives about life on earth and what really matters to me when using this exercise. This is a nice way to trick yourself into being real with how you feel apart from self judgement. Practice this mental framing exercise whenever you find it difficult to get answers about your perspective. You can also record your dreams in a dream journal for later examination. Dreams have been known to be symbolic references of our inner world. Getting in touch with your dream life is a topic we will discuss later.

Once you've put together your list of core beliefs, it's time to start working on them. This may be a rather long process, but the payoff is immense. There are two powerful ways you can hack your mind and get the results you want out of life. These steps alone with cause you to start seeing a change in your quality of life and overall happiness. The first way to alter one's belief system is to use Affirmations and self-talk.

The Scientific Evidence

The use of simple mnemonics may seem trivial but there is MRI evidence that suggests the ventromedial prefrontal cortex—involved in positive valuation and self-related information processing—becomes more active when we think positively about ourselves. During Self affirmation these neural pathways are increased. Based on the results of a study done by Falk and colleagues, we can see that when we practice positive affirmations, we're better able to see "otherwise-threatening information as more self-relevant and valuable".

I've been using affirmations for many years to induce lucid dreams, astral projection experiences, and improve my mental health. It's important to note here that the goal of self-talk and positive affirmations is to plant a message within the subconscious mind. Doing this can be rather difficult due to the left hemisphere of the brain acting as a logical and analytical gatekeeper of information and belief systems. Simply saying to yourself "I am happy and healthy," before bed isn't really going to be enough. Given, this will have some positive effect, it won't be as potent as other techniques. To communicate best with the subconscious mind, we must first know it's language.

Connection to The Subconscious

To the surprise of many, the subconscious mind doesn't speak with words. You may be wondering how affirmations work then. The subconscious mind communicates through feelings and symbolic imagery. The proverbial saying "a picture is worth a thousand words," is the right idea. The subconscious mind takes in information in a nonlinear and multidimensional way, which is then processed and flattened from its original abstract nature to something that makes more sense to our conscious minds. Affirmations with the adage of mental imagery are much more effective. For instance, if you wanted to break a smoking habit, you'd say something like "I only put healthy things into my body and avoid smoking cigarettes." You would then pair that affirmation with the mental image of you eating a healthy salad or refusing a cigarette offered to you. The combination of affirmations and images communicates your desires much more effectively to your subconscious.

It is also a good practice to add a period of thankfulness and elevated moods to the end of your affirmation session. Spend some time feeling how healthy your new body is, and how happy your loved ones are about your decision to stop smoking. Feeling the reality you seek to manifest will connect your vibration to it and bring it to you much faster. In my daily spiritual practice, I use affirmations like spells. I read them many times in both past, present, and future tense, then visualize the result I want. I refer to them as spells because I use them to activate my psychic abilities and facilitate powerful change within me. I encourage you to do the same. If you long to awaken your psychic abilities, create a positive affirmation about the specific ability you want to operate in. This process of affecting mental change through affirmation is a rather slow method and may take anywhere from a few weeks to a few months to show results.

Connecting The Current

This is because our old habits and patterns of belief have been established nearly our entire lives. Uprooting these negative ideologies will take time and effort. Visualization will be a skill that takes a long time to get the hang of. Mental imagery can be developed like any other skill and is one of the foundations of psychic work and magic. This is true especially for more advanced practices like astral projection. That fact may be discouraging, but mastery of the basics will make the advanced skills seem easy. You wouldn't try learning guitar by first trying to play a song by led zeppelin. You'd start with the basics of chord shapes and progression. Until you were finally able to play your first song. Spiritual growth works in much the same way. You must start with the rudimentary skills like meditation, visualization, and affirmations, before you can move on to seeing chakras, manipulating energy, and eventually astral projecting and working magic.

Chapter 11

The Ancient Way to Astral Travel

When tracing the origins of Astral Projection, we are led back thousands of years, to ancient civilizations steeped in spiritual wisdom often ignored. Their philosophies and understanding of life and the afterlife often bore fundamental principles that resonate with modern Astral Projection practices. As we peel back the layers of history, we find ourselves amidst the grandeur of the ancient Egyptian civilization and the profound wisdom of Indian spirituality.

Connecting The Current

The eminent mystic and scholar Manly P. Hall, in his book "The Secret Teachings of All Ages," dives into this concept. He states, "The Egyptians believed that the soul, leaving the body at death, could function in the physical world as well as in several superphysical states of being." This belief laid the foundation for practices similar to Astral Projection.

To understand this quote deeply, we need to grasp the Egyptian perspective on life and the afterlife. For the ancient Egyptians, death was not an end, but rather a transition into another state of existence. The 'ka,' being immortal, was believed to navigate these various states of existence, functioning independently of the physical body. This ability to consciously navigate different realms and dimensions closely aligns with what we understand as Astral Projection today.

Ancient Roots of Astral Travel

The ancient Egyptians had a rich spiritual framework that encompassed concepts akin to Astral Projection. Their civilization, flourishing alongside the Nile for over three millennia, harbored a complex belief system centered around the idea of life, death, and the afterlife. In this spiritual framework, the 'ka,' or the 'spirit-double,' was of immense significance. The 'ka' was considered a part of the individual that would continue to exist even after death. It was believed to have the ability to move freely between realms, inhabit other dimensions, and even communicate with gods. I'll go into more detail on this later.

In a practical sense, the ancient Egyptians performed elaborate rituals to aid this journey of the 'ka.' Death was seen as a profound spiritual journey, and tombs were often filled with texts, known as the Pyramid Texts and later, the Book of the Dead, to guide the 'ka' on its journey. These texts provided instructions, spells and maps to navigate the spiritual realm, akin to a manual for Astral Projection. Through these practices, the ancient Egyptians demonstrated an early understanding of the freedom of the soul or consciousness from the physical body.

Moving eastwards, ancient Indian spiritual traditions also held profound understandings about the nature of the soul and its transcendental abilities. The Upanishads, ancient Indian texts that explore deep philosophical concepts, reference the 'atman' or the individual soul's ability to traverse beyond physical reality.

In the Upanishads, three states of consciousness are discussed: waking (jagrat), dreaming (swapna), and deep sleep (sushupti). 'Swapna,' the dream state, is particularly interesting when considering Astral Projection. It is in this state that the 'atman' or the individual soul is considered to be free from the physical confines, experiencing realities beyond the tangible world. This concept strongly aligns with the experience of Astral Projection, where the astral body or consciousness separates from the physical body to traverse astral planes.

Within the practice of Yoga, particularly in the path of Raja Yoga, meditators seek to consciously access and explore these states. Techniques involving focused concentration, visualization, and breath control are used to transition from the waking state to the dream state without losing consciousness, thereby inducing a state akin to Astral Projection. For instance, the practice of Yoga Nidra or 'yogic sleep' involves a deep relaxation technique where the practitioner maintains a state of consciousness between wakefulness and sleep, often resulting in experiences similar to Astral Projection.

Unraveling these ancient roots offers us invaluable insights into the timeless nature of Astral Projection. It connects us to the wisdom of our ancestors and enriches our understanding of this practice. As we journey forward, we carry with us this accumulated wisdom, learning from the experiences of those who walked this path before us, and paving our own path towards deeper understanding and spiritual growth.

The Secret of The Astral Echo

Despite the historical significance and cultural ubiquity of Astral Projection, it has been encrusted with an array of myths and misconceptions over time. One widespread fear is the idea of not being able to return to one's physical body, becoming permanently lost in the astral realm. This myth has probably stemmed from fear of the unknown, a natural human tendency. However, seasoned practitioners and experts in the field assert that the silver cord, an energetic tether linking the astral body to the physical body, ensures the safe return of the projector. The astral cord plays a very important role in communicating with the divine.

Connection is the engine behind magic and is the source of our very life. With it, all things are possible. Astral traveling is but a biproduct of connection. Ever spiritual practice can be regarded as a pursuit of connection. To understand this abiding for, it helps to know where it comes from. I call it source but there are many names for it, most commonly named God. From source a cord connects us from our higher selves, our closest expression of light, to our physically bodies, and there are astral bodies or echoes that reside in the realms between. We are connected to source through the astral cord. It is a myth to believe that the astral cord is merely a safety string stopping you from floating away from your physical body while astral traveling. Many such powerful ideas are watered down thus depriving us of their intended meaning. The astral cord is central to our experience of consciousness all together. Without it we wouldn't be here at all.

The astral cord acts as the umbilicus for life force energy. The cord is the channel by which connection is felt. I was amazed with this revelation when I experienced it firsthand. The experience where I saw what I thought was an angel, was actually my astral echo, what the Egyptians called the Ka. It lives and evolves just as we do in this physical reality. When you manifest or command things into being through magic, it is the astral echo that brings the result to you. Think of this as the universal courier service. When you pray or perform rituals and ask God for answers or protection, the astral echo conveys those messages. It is your etheric counterpart. Many people struggle with astral projection and magic in general because they have yet to connect with the first spirit. In many occult circles this spirit has been called holy guardian angel, the spirit given charge of you at birth.

The Astral Plane

Another popular misconception revolves around the fear of encountering malevolent entities or spirits while projecting. This fear, while understandable given our human instinct to be wary of unseen forces, is largely baseless. In his seminal work "Astral Dynamics," Robert Bruce, a respected authority in the field, assures readers that the astral plane is not a haunted realm filled with malevolent spirits, but a playground for the spirit. He writes, "Although it is natural to fear the unknown, especially the kind of unknown you may face during astral projection, fear itself is quite unjustified. No harm will come to you during your astral adventures." It's comforting to know that our astral adventures need not be tinged with fear and trepidation.

The Astral Plane is a concept as fascinating as the practice itself. While it may sound like something out of a sci-fi novel, the Astral Plane is a non-physical realm of existence, parallel to our physical world, and accessible through Astral Projection. It's a different dimension that Astral Projectors describe as vibrantly alive and teeming with entities and energies that exist beyond our usual sensory perception.

One of the most influential figures in the field of Astral Projection, Robert Monroe, gives an immersive description of the Astral Plane in his groundbreaking book "Journeys Out of the Body." He explains, "The astral plane is not an 'out there' but an 'in here.' It is a very real non-physical world or dimension of life that exists along with the physical world, but at a different frequency of consciousness." Monroe's description implies that the Astral Plane, although non-physical, is as real and concrete to its inhabitants as our world is to us. This understanding expands our concept of reality, suggesting that existence extends beyond the physical realm we perceive in our day-to-day lives.

While astral projection is a deeply spiritual practice, it also holds immense psychological significance. It provides a gateway into the depths of our minds, bringing us face-to-face with our subconscious thoughts and emotions. This can facilitate a profound understanding of our inner selves, aiding in personal development and emotional growth. British author and researcher Oliver Fox, in his book "Astral Projection: A Record of Out-of-Body Experiences," discusses the psychological implications of astral projection. He proposes that "The astral dream state... enables us to come into direct contact with the deeper levels of our unconscious and makes these available for investigation." Fox's viewpoint suggests that Astral Projection can be an invaluable tool for introspection and self-exploration, serving as a bridge between our conscious and unconscious minds.

Though astral projection is often pursued for spiritual enlightenment and personal growth, it can also bestow numerous physical and emotional benefits upon practitioners. Regular practice of Astral Projection can result in stress relief, improved sleep quality, heightened intuition, an enhanced sense of empathy, and a more profound understanding of oneself and the universe.

Robert Peterson, in his book "Out-of-Body Experiences: How to Have Them and What to Expect," elaborates on these benefits. He states, "OBEs (Out-of-Body Experiences) can offer considerable benefits: increased self-awareness, answers to religious questions, increased psychic abilities, a decreased fear of death, healing, and even happiness." As Peterson underlines, Astral Projection serves as a conduit for holistic personal and spiritual growth, with the potential to bring about positive change in various aspects of our lives.

Universal Consciousness

It's essential to acknowledge the diversity of approaches that exist. Techniques for astral projection vary widely, reflecting the rich tapestry of cultural and individual experiences that contribute to this practice. From meditative states in ancient Buddhist traditions to the dream work practices of indigenous cultures, Astral Projection encompasses a broad spectrum of methods.

Out of body travel has recently found its way into the realm of scientific exploration. Researchers are attempting to elucidate the phenomenon using concepts from quantum mechanics and consciousness studies. For example, the theory of quantum entanglement, which posits that particles can be interconnected regardless of the physical distance between them, offers intriguing parallels to the experience of astral projection.

Simultaneously, consciousness research offers fascinating insights. Dr. Stuart Hameroff, in his book "Quantum Consciousness," suggests that consciousness is not simply a by-product of the brain but rather a fundamental feature of the universe that may extend beyond our physical selves. These scientific perspectives validate spiritual experiences, serving to bridge the divide between the two. Still, it's essential to remember that Astral Projection is, at its core, a personal and experiential practice. As William Buhlman put it, "The exploration of the afterlife and non-physical realities is a personal adventure of discovery. Only firsthand experience provides true knowledge." Thus, the melding of scientific theory and personal experience is what truly enriches our understanding of Astral Projection.

Astral Projection & Lucid Dreaming

A common point of confusion in discussions about altered states of consciousness is the distinction between astral projection and lucid dreaming. While both involve a heightened state of consciousness, they are fundamentally different experiences. Lucid dreaming refers to the awareness of being in a dream state and the ability to control one's actions within the dream. On the other hand, Astral Projection involves a conscious experience of one's astral body departing from their physical form to explore the astral plane. Robert Monroe presents a clear distinction: "Lucid dreams occur within the confines of the physical body, while Astral Projection occurs when consciousness is directed outside the physical body." This quote underlines the primary difference between the two – the locus of consciousness.

In Astral Projection, practitioners report experiencing a clear departure from their physical bodies and a vivid exploration of different astral realms. In contrast, lucid dreaming is typically characterized by surreal and dream-like qualities but lacks the sensation of consciously leaving the body.

The Fractal Universe

Separation is the illusion and is simultaneously our liberation from it. The journey of the little soul or animula is the process of utilizing the concepts we've seen through this book. It is the process of inner alchemy, the transforming of base metals into gold, earth into heaven. Astral projection is our key. It liberates us from the chains that bind us both mentally and physically. To be free from this world is a blessing that is the birthright of us all. You must break free and, like Neo in the matrix, you must be born again. The greater mysteries of reality are presented plainly in the paradox of mind over matter. Ask yourself this: does it matter if you have actually left this reality and journeyed to another in spirit, or if your mind just created the experience for you? That's a deeper question that it may at first seem. I think the structure of this reality resembles the essence of that question. Some believe that life at every level of existence is the extended dream of God or source consciousness. So, does it matter if you've traveled beyond the body in an objective sense? The answer might shock you. No.

If that answer frustrates something central to your identity, you've found the root to your problem of perpetual enslavement to this illusion. Consider the nature of a dream as we've spoken about before. However, this time think about the feeling of waking up from that dream, how real it was while you lived it. I've had powerful dreams that lasted what felt like lifetimes. I've had families, friends, and very real aspirations. But those dreams inevitably faded to this more persistent reality. Every time I thought to myself, how is it possible to experience two lives simultaneously? How can I live in another world and still come back to this world, both in their claiming to be real in their seasons?

This reality betrays itself by its fractal nature. If you want to be free of your corporal prison, to dance free of physical weight, and be bound by thought alone, you must take this concept to heart. You are more than your body. "Yes, Cal, you said that already." I know. But it is the truth. This reality is fractal and so reveals in the smallest thing, the grandest of mysteries. Life is the sort of thing that requires you know every bit of it just to understand the simplest thing. The dream state, the lives lived behind closed eyes, expose the nature of this game. While you dream you may be completely convinced you are in objective reality. You would bet your life on it. Funny enough, I often did just that. I started to test the boundaries of the dream world and I found it hollow and wanting.

Beneath us all, deep within, we are hungry, we are passionately seeking the abrupt cessation of this dream. We want to wake up back home in the light. I began to feel this sadness, this lack and want for more even in my dreams. For a season of my life I wept in my dreams. Not for any discernable reason. Now I know I was broken because I could not get free of this game. That longing for home is felt in this reality as well, and what is the difference between the two? How can we say this world is real? What at all is this strange concept of real and why on earth does it matter to a being that hallucinates every moment of its time here?

The Most Powerful Method For Astral Project

Ultimately, connection is the sweetest freedom. It is the fulfillment of our hopes and the certainty of our return to the light. And thus, astral travel is a natural biproduct of uncovering the trick of reality. The experiences you are having now is no different from the ones you have while you are sleeping. The power of the mind to create worlds of infinite number is proof of your inherent godhood. You've dreamt this world as you do the dream worlds. This is why it doesn't matter if you've actually teleported to another dimension or if you're mind merely produced that experience. Before you move to crucify me for this concept, understand that I'm not dismissing the very real nature of astral projection and magic as a whole. With enough power and control, intention alone can alter reality. There are in fact beings that reside in higher realms that watch us and guide us. I'll talk more about them later.

Breaking this final barrier will make astral travel and any other act of magic rather natural and easy. Free your mind of the burden of confinement to the rules of this reality. It isn't at all your natural state of being. We are only aware of our place in this reality because we trust our five senses over our more subtle senses. Your natural state is boundlessness. You exist in a state of limitless possibility. If you search within yourself you've see that this is true. Place a hand on your heart and just feel. Do nothing else, do strive or contrive, just wait. Waiting brings with it the expectation for more and the freedom from limits. Just wait and see what happens. If you're silent you'll hear it—the little voice whispering, "wake up."

This is by far the most powerful method for astral projection. Just wait and know, I mean truly *know* what you seek will be yours. The mind is so powerful, so beyond bounds and barriers that if you wait and know, you will see and experience. Your prison is only powered by your disbelief. This is why Jesus only ever told the disciples to have faith. I can prescribe many techniques and methods to help you to have an out of body experience but there are thousands of books out there that do that. Methods are bars and techniques are cages. They serve only to reinforce a narrative of bondage. When I set out to astral project, I say to myself, it is time. I want this and it will be. I understand that I exist in several realities simultaneously. I am no more bound here than I am in a dream. The methods and techniques are useful in the beginning, but as with all things, they must too be let go.

Connecting The Current

The state of connection and ascension is a practice of letting go. Giving up who you believe you are so you can receive who you actually are. We live our lives holding on to an idea of life with clenched fists, unable to take hold of the truth. You must let go to take hold, relinquish power to gain it, die to truly live. In that way, life takes on a mesmerizing beauty and beguiling grace. We are connected by threads so fine and subtle they may not be said to exist at all, but for the acutely sensitive, the bonds between us are felt.

Connection eludes most. Some go their whole lives without ever tapping into the fullness of it. It pervades and consumes us all. It is the life that echoes forth from every corner of the infinite. Connection is what Jesus taught. It is how he healed the sick and raised the dead. It is the way back home, like a porch light left on at night. It goes beyond words or the need to speak at all. When connection is felt this world fades to static and gives way to a more vibrant transmission. Connection feels like chills, like goosebumps and swelling emotion in the heart center. If you learn nothing else in this life, learn to abide in connection, the ever flowing current of divine presence.

The Astral Echo

We are temples for the living god. This is what my astral echo was saying when I saw it the night of my first encounter. When it touched me and lightening shot through me and I levitated it vanished. This happened because it merged with me. From that moment on I astral projected easily and often times rather effortlessly. It felt natural like navigating your room in the dark. I knew what the astral plane was because I had been there all my life. The physical body is a vessel made for this realm, whereas the astral echo is made to traverse the etheric realms.

Though we are connected to source, the strength of this connection is weak in most people. It's only after the astral echo connects with them that they have an awakening and see the matrix for what it is. This is where meditation comes it. It strengthens that connection and improves the clarity of communication between us and the divine. When I merged with my astral echo my psychic abilities leveled up. Suddenly I was predicting events, seeing angel numbers everywhere I looked, and astral projecting daily. This is the right of passage talked about in ancient grimoires like The Book of Abramelin. The holy guardian angel is mentioned several places in the bible to describe the way angels protect us. In ancient grimoires, connecting with the holy guardian angel was a lengthy, arduous process that involved months of meditation and purification to align the practitioner with their divine will, resulting in an experience of the divine. Prior to my encounter with the astral echo, I had been fasting, praying, and dedicating myself to worship and meditation. Only after months of this did I meet my guardian angel.

Having worked with spirits for several years, I see that most people have issues because they haven't merged with their astral echo. Spirits withhold contact when they see a person isn't spiritually developed enough to interact with them energetically. There's no getting around it, you must merge with the astral echo if you want to connect with divine beings. Afterall this is the whole point of astral projection. From this view, projection isn't your spirit leaving your body, it is the transferal of your conscious mind into the astral echo.

The astral echo acts as a preliminary guide that ushers you through the astral realm. It is often the voice people report hearing while out of body. It is the logos that speaks during intense psychedelic trips. It was the entity that pulled me out of body the first time I astral projected. The powers and possibilities of the astral echo are many. The most surprising of them for most people is splitting the consciousness. In other words, making a double of yourself. While out of body it is possible to split oneself into several parts. Once you've returned to your body, the astral copies you've made continue to do work in the astral plane, communing with spirits, manifesting your desires, and building your energies. At the end of every day, I receive these copies back into myself and with them the memories and experiences as well. At first this can be an incredibly disorienting process and requires a great deal of focus, but with time this ability grants a new expansiveness of consciousness.

Chapter 12

The Divine Guides and Kundalini

The source of true magic, as understood by the ancient texts, lies in the spirit that supplies the power. This spirit, or divine essence, is the force that animates all living things and connects them to the greater cosmos. By aligning oneself with this divine essence through ritual and intention, one can tap into a wellspring of infinite potential and wisdom. The Egyptians were not merely practitioners of an esoteric art but custodians of a profound spiritual legacy. Their rituals and practices offer a glimpse into a world where the boundaries between the mortal and the divine were fluid, and where humans could commune with gods and harness their power for the greater good.

Connecting The Current

Many cultures and belief systems have roots that lead back to Egyptian methodologies. Looking deeper into the connections between ancient cultures reveals similar origins and other worldly encounters. Some of the most prevalent shared myths are the flood myths which appear in nearly all ancient cultures. These stories, though separated by vast distances and differences in tradition, share striking similarities that suggest a common origin or a universal human experience.

Recent scientific evidence suggests that such an event did indeed occur, fundamentally reshaping our understanding of ancient history. This discovery opens the door to the possibility that many other shared stories from ancient cultures may also hold truths we have yet to uncover, hindered largely by the lack of funding and resources. The ruling class elite, the so-called one percent who control the world's wealth, bear significant responsibility for the dismissal and neglect of these important inquiries.

Geological studies have provided compelling evidence that a massive flood event occurred around 5600 BCE. Researchers have discovered sedimentary layers and water marks that indicate a rapid and significant rise in sea levels, consistent with the timeline of the Great Flood. One such finding is the presence of marine fossils far inland and at high elevations, which suggests that these areas were once submerged under water. Additionally, analysis of ancient sediments from the Black Sea region reveals a sudden influx of saltwater, supporting the hypothesis of a catastrophic flooding event that transformed the freshwater lake into a saltwater sea

Investigating Common Themes

If the Great Flood, once considered a myth, can be substantiated through scientific inquiry, it stands to reason that other ancient stories might also be rooted in historical events. Many cultures share narratives of creation, celestial beings, and significant transformative events that shaped human civilization. Yet, these stories are often dismissed by mainstream science, which is heavily influenced by the priorities and interests of the ruling elite. The one percent, who control vast amounts of wealth and resources, have little incentive to invest in research that could challenge the established narratives that underpin their power.

The lack of funding for archaeological and anthropological research into ancient myths and legends is a direct consequence of this control. Discoveries that could revolutionize our understanding of human history are stifled, not because they lack merit, but because they threaten the status quo. Mesopotamia stands as a testament to humanity's earliest attempts to understand and interact with the divine. Nestled between the Tigris and Euphrates rivers, this ancient land was home to some of the earliest known cities, complex societies, and written languages. It is here, in the fertile crescent, that we find the first whispers of spirit magic—a tradition that bridges the mundane and the mystical, guiding humanity through the ages.

The Enuma Elish, the Babylonian creation epic that dates back to the second millennium BCE is more than a mere creation story; it is a profound allegory of cosmic order, divine intervention, and the interplay between gods and humans. The Enuma Elish provides a foundational understanding of how ancient civilizations perceived their gods and the unseen forces that shaped their world. In the beginning, there was chaos. The Enuma Elish opens with a world submerged in primordial waters, where the freshwaters of Apsu and the salt waters of Tiamat commingled. From this chaotic union emerged the first gods. As these deities multiplied and became more complex, they disturbed the primal waters, leading to conflict and the eventual rise of the god Marduk.

Marduk's ascent to supremacy is marked by his battle with Tiamat, the embodiment of chaos. With his divine powers, Marduk defeats Tiamat and fashions the heavens and the earth from her divided body. This act of creation is not just a physical transformation but a metaphysical one, representing the imposition of order over chaos. The Enuma Elish, therefore, is a narrative of divine intervention where gods actively shape the cosmos and establish the principles of existence.

The gods of Mesopotamia were not distant, abstract entities but active participants in the world's affairs.

They intervened in human lives, guiding, protecting, and sometimes punishing those who deviated from the divine order. This concept of divine intervention is a recurring theme across various cultures and religions, emphasizing the idea that humanity is under the watchful eyes of higher powers.

One of the most significant figures in Mesopotamian spirituality is the god Enki the deity of wisdom, magic. Enki's role as a mediator between the gods and humans is pivotal. He is often depicted as a benefactor of humanity, providing them with sacred knowledge and guidance used to bring forth great change.

Divine Intervention

This idea of harnessing divine power through sacred knowledge is echoed in many other cultures. In ancient Egypt, for instance, the god Thoth played a similar role. Known as the scribe of the gods, Thoth was the keeper of the divine laws and the mediator between the celestial and terrestrial realms. His teachings, encapsulated in texts such as the Emerald Tablet, reveal the principles of alchemy, magic, and spiritual transformation.

The Vedas and Upanishads provide profound insights into the nature of reality and the human soul in similar ways. The Rigveda's Nasadiya Sukta, also known as the Hymn of Creation, ponders the origins of the universe and the mysterious forces that govern it. This hymn, with its poetic contemplation of existence, mirrors the

Mesopotamian quest for understanding the divine order.

In the Rigveda, the creation of the universe is described as emerging from a state of non-being, where neither existence nor non-existence prevailed. This primordial void, akin to the chaotic waters of Tiamat, is the source from which all things arise. The Rigveda's exploration of cosmic origins emphasizes the interconnectedness of all creation and the presence of divine forces that shape the world.

The idea of divine intervention is further elaborated in the epics of Ramayana and Mahabharata. In the Ramayana, the god Vishnu incarnates as Prince Rama to restore dharma (cosmic order) by defeating the demon king Ravana. Throughout his journey, Rama is aided by various divine beings, including Hanuman, the monkey god, who symbolizes unwavering devotion and spiritual strength. The Ramayana's narrative of divine assistance and heroic struggle underscores the belief in a higher power guiding and protecting humanity.

Similarly, the Mahabharata, with its intricate tales of gods, heroes, and moral dilemmas, illustrates the principle of divine intervention. The Bhagavad Gita, a pivotal part of the Mahabharata, features the god Krishna imparting spiritual wisdom to Prince Arjuna on the battlefield of Kurukshetra. Krishna's guidance, emphasizing duty, righteousness, and the eternal nature of the soul, reflects the timeless truths found in various spiritual traditions. These ancient texts and epics, though distinct in their cultural contexts, share common themes of divine intervention and the connection between humans and higher powers. They reveal a universal quest for understanding the mysteries of existence and the role of divine beings in guiding humanity.

The overlap of these themes across different religions highlights the idea that all spiritual traditions are variations on a common theme. Whether it is Enki imparting the sacred law to humanity, Thoth recording the divine laws, or Krishna guiding Arjuna, the message is clear: there are higher forces at play, and through knowledge and devotion, humans can align themselves with these forces.

Connecting With The Divine Council

The concept of divine intervention is not limited to ancient texts but extends to the spiritual practices of today. Modern mystics and spiritual seekers continue to explore the connection between the physical and spiritual realms. Practices such as meditation, prayer, and ritual magic are tools for accessing the divine and harnessing spiritual energy.

One of the most intriguing aspects of these practices is the use of symbols and rituals to invoke divine presence. In Mesopotamian spirituality, rituals played a crucial role in maintaining harmony between the gods and humans. The priests, acting as intermediaries, performed elaborate ceremonies to honor the gods and ensure their favor. These rituals often involved the use of sacred symbols, chants, and offerings, creating a bridge between the material and spiritual worlds.

This tradition of using symbols and rituals to connect with the divine is seen in many other cultures. In ancient Egypt, rituals involving the use of hieroglyphs, sacred chants, and offerings were central to the practice of magic. The hieroglyphs themselves were considered powerful symbols, capable of influencing the spiritual realm. Similarly, in Hinduism, the use of mantras (sacred sounds) and yantras (sacred diagrams) in rituals serves to invoke the presence of deities and align the practitioner with divine energy.

The power of symbols and rituals lies in their ability to focus the mind and channel spiritual energy. By engaging in these practices, one can transcend the limitations of the physical body and access higher states of consciousness. This is the essence of spirit magic—the ability to influence the unseen forces that shape our reality. In the context of the divine council, these practices are the tools that enable us to connect with the higher beings who govern the cosmos. The rituals and symbols serve as maps and guides, leading the seeker through the inner landscape to the realm of the divine.

The Ascended Masters

The journey to connect with the divine council is not a solitary endeavor but one that requires guidance and support. Throughout history, figures such as Jesus, Buddha, and Mahavatar Babaji have acted as intermediaries, conveying the teachings of the divine to humanity. These enlightened masters received their insights through direct communion with higher beings, embodying the principles of spirit magic in their lives and teachings.

The story of Mahavatar Babaji, a revered figure in the Kriya Yoga tradition, exemplifies this connection. Babaji is believed to be an immortal yogi who has guided many spiritual seekers throughout the ages. His teachings, passed down through his disciples, emphasize the importance of meditation, breath control, and the awakening of the spiritual energy known as kundalini. Babaji's guidance, like that of the divine council, provides a path for those seeking to transcend the material world and achieve spiritual enlightenment.

The teachings of these enlightened masters, though rooted in specific cultural and religious contexts, share a common thread: the belief in the possibility of direct communication with the divine. This communication is facilitated through practices such as meditation, prayer, and ritual magic, which serve to attune the practitioner to the higher frequencies of the spiritual realm.

The Mystery of The Tree of Life

Of the many shared teachings given by these masters, the motif of the Tree of Life emerges in various cultures and religious traditions, each imbued with profound symbolism and esoteric wisdom. From the ancient Mesopotamian flood myths to the diverse pantheons of gods and spiritual practices, the Tree of Life serves as a potent allegory for the interconnectedness of life, the cosmos, and the divine.

The earliest depictions of the Tree of Life can be traced back to the Mesopotamian civilizations, where it is often associated with the divine and the afterlife. The Sumerians, for example, depicted the sacred tree in the myth of Gilgamesh, where it is seen as a source of eternal life and wisdom. In the Babylonian Epic of Gilgamesh, the hero seeks the plant of immortality, which is rooted in the depths of the ocean, symbolizing the connection between the earthly and the divine. Similarly, the Assyrians depicted the Tree of Life in their art and mythology, often guarded by divine beings such as the winged genies. These representations highlight the tree as a symbol of divine knowledge and the interconnectedness of all creation.

In the Judaic tradition, the Tree of Life is prominently featured in the Garden of Eden story within the Torah. The tree is depicted as a source of eternal life, juxtaposed with the Tree of Knowledge of Good and Evil. The Kabbalistic interpretation of the Tree of Life further deepens its significance, presenting it as a mystical diagram that maps out the ten sefirot (emanations) through which the divine manifests in the world.

Kabbalists view the Tree of Life as a representation of the human soul and the universe, offering a path to spiritual enlightenment and union with the divine. The ten sefirot correspond to different aspects of God and the human psyche, reflecting the intricate relationship between the physical and the spiritual realms.

In Hinduism, the concept of the Tree of Life is mirrored in the sacred fig tree, or the Bodhi tree, under which Siddhartha Gautama attained enlightenment and became the Buddha. This tree symbolizes the interconnectedness of all life and the pathway to spiritual awakening. The chakra system in Hinduism also parallels the Tree of Life, with the seven chakras representing different energy centers in the human body. These chakras are often visualized as lotuses or trees, with the kundalini energy lying dormant at the base of the spine. When awakened, the kundalini rises through these chakras, activating each one and culminating in the union with the divine consciousness.

In Norse mythology, Yggdrasil, the World Tree, is a colossal ash tree that connects the nine worlds, including Asgard (the realm of the gods) and Midgard (the realm of humans). Yggdrasil is the axis mundi, the cosmic axis that holds the universe together, and is a source of wisdom and life. The Well of Urd, located at the base of Yggdrasil, is where the Norns reside, and it is from this well that the tree draws its sustenance. This imagery signifies the deep connection between fate, life, and the divine, underscoring the tree's role as a bridge between worlds.

Across these diverse traditions, the Tree of Life serves as a powerful allegory for the chakra system. Just as the Tree of Life connects the heavens and the earth, the chakras also connect the physical body with the spiritual realms. The chakras, when activated, allow for the flow of prana (life force) through the body, leading to spiritual awakening and enlightenment. The sacred secretion, often referred to as the "nectar of immortality" in esoteric traditions, is believed to be a divine fluid that flows within the human body. In yogic practices, this nectar is associated with the amrita or soma, which is said to drip from the pineal gland when the kundalini energy is awakened. This process is akin to the sap that flows through the Tree of Life, nourishing and sustaining it.

The Allegory of The Garden

In the Garden of Eden, the serpent tempts Adam and Eve to eat from the Tree of Knowledge of Good and Evil, promising them divine wisdom. Traditionally viewed as a tale of temptation and fall, this story can be reinterpreted through a spiritual lens, where the serpent represents the kundalini energy coiled at the base of the spine.

The Tree of Life in the garden symbolizes the chakra system, with its roots in the earth (the base chakra) and its branches reaching up to the heavens (the crown chakra). As the kundalini serpent awakens and ascends the spine, it travels through the chakras, activating each energy center and bringing about a heightened state of consciousness.

Eating the fruit from the Tree of Knowledge represents the culmination of the kundalini's ascent and the realization of divine consciousness. This allegory illustrates the transformative power of spiritual awakening, where the individual transcends ordinary human limitations and attains a higher state of being.

In this enlightened state, one gains profound insights into the nature of reality, experiences a deep connection with the divine, and understands the interconnectedness of all life. This is the ultimate realization that all major religions and spiritual traditions aim for, symbolized by the Tree of Life. The kundalini energy, when awakened, allows one to access this inner wisdom and connect with the divine.

The Kundalini & Dualism

The common thread across these religious and mystical traditions is the belief that true communication with the gods occurs when the kundalini is activated. Kundalini, derived from the Sanskrit word "kundal," meaning coiled, refers to the dormant energy at the base of the spine. When awakened through spiritual practices such as meditation, yoga, or ritual, this energy rises through the chakras, leading to profound spiritual experiences and direct communion with the divine. In the Gnostic tradition, this concept is echoed in the idea of gnosis, or direct knowledge of the divine. Gnostics believed that true spiritual enlightenment could only be achieved through personal experience and inner revelation, often facilitated by the activation of the kundalini. In the traditional interpretation, eating the fruit from the Tree of Knowledge of Good and Evil introduced sin into the world, marking the fall of humankind. This binary framework of good versus evil has been a cornerstone in many religious teachings, promoting the idea that human actions must align with a defined moral code to avoid divine punishment.

By establishing a clear boundary between good and evil, religious and societal structures have been able to exert control over individuals. The fear of punishment and the promise of reward compel people to conform to specific behaviors and beliefs, often without questioning the underlying truths. This system of control diverts individuals from seeking personal spiritual experiences and understanding the deeper mysteries of existence.

Esoteric traditions reveal that true spiritual enlightenment transcends the simplistic duality of good and evil. The ultimate truth is neither inherently good nor bad; it is a state of being that encompasses all aspects of existence without judgment. This perspective aligns with the teachings of many mystics and philosophers who advocate for a holistic understanding of reality. When Adam and Eve ate from the Tree of

Knowledge, they gained awareness, not just of good and evil, but of the complexities and nuances of existence. This act symbolizes the awakening of consciousness and the beginning of a journey towards self-realization and divine understanding.

The activation of kundalini energy allows us to rise above the dualistic concepts of good and evil. As the kundalini ascends through the chakras, it awakens a higher state of consciousness, enabling one to perceive the interconnectedness and unity of all things. This spiritual awakening leads to an experiential understanding of truth, unclouded by moralistic judgments. This frees us from the ego entirely. This is what Jesus means when he commands us to love each other like we love ourselves. He goes on to save we are all one, connected with God. To abide in Jesus is to abide in the energy, the presence he walked in, the current of the divine.

By moving beyond the myth of good and evil, we embrace the true nature of reality—one that is dynamic, interconnected, and ever-evolving. This shift in perspective frees us from the constraints of imposed beliefs and opens the path to genuine spiritual growth. It encourages us to seek knowledge and enlightenment through personal experience and inner transformation, rather than adhering to externally imposed doctrines.

Chapter 13

How To Enter Heaven

Awakening to true spiritual reality is a strange ordeal. Many find themselves trapped in the minutiae of this societal system, and others are swept away by every sensational idea that comes their way. People new to the path are as vulnerable as sea turtle hatchlings that must dodge every kind of predator to reach safety the moment they are born. The potential pitfalls are quite numerous for those beginning their journey. This is not the way it is supposed to be. Our society doesn't nurture the spiritual newborn. It does much the opposite, acting to stifle any kind of internal flight toward source. This is the established order that Jesus fought against. This force seeks to separate man from God, and to replace presences with a pulpit. The only solution is violence. Not with physicality but by taking the kingdom by force.

Many of the ancient texts and sacred scriptures I've introduced in this book have had the ticket of allegory tagged to them. And for the most part that remains true. However, to take the information I've given without means or motive to act upon them is the deepest kind of folly. Though these epics and stories of gods and men are often shown through the light of symbolism and parable, they have real application. After all, as within so without. The entities of old and the beings talked about throughout antiquity are very much real, yet without a mastery of the inner universe you'll never encounter them lest you use violent means.

The Kingdom Suffers Violence

In the Gospel of Matthew 11:12, Jesus makes a profound and enigmatic statement: "From the days of John the Baptist until now, the kingdom of heaven suffers violence, and the violent take it by force." This verse has been the subject of extensive theological debate and interpretation. My theory is that this passage speaks to the aggressive pursuit of spiritual enlightenment and the transformative power of accessing the divine within ourselves. This can be seen as analogous to modern practices such as the use of psychedelics, magic, and sensory deprivation to tap into the hidden realms of the mind.

The phrase "the kingdom of heaven suffers violence" can be understood as a metaphor for the intense and often tumultuous journey of spiritual awakening. Traditional interpretations often focus on the idea that the kingdom of heaven is under assault from forces of evil or that people are fervently striving to enter it.

However, from a mystical perspective, this "violence" can be seen as the forceful breaking through of the barriers of ordinary consciousness to access higher states of awareness.

In the context of modern spiritual practices, psychedelics, magic, and sensory deprivation can be viewed as tools that help individuals break through these barriers. Psychedelics, such as psilocybin mushrooms, LSD, and ayahuasca, have been used for centuries in various cultures for their profound mind-altering effects. These substances can induce states of consciousness that allow individuals to experience a sense of unity with the divine, encounter spiritual entities, and gain insights into the nature of reality. This process is often described as a journey inward, where the mind becomes the theater of divine revelation.

Magic, particularly in the form of ritual and ceremonial practices, involves the intentional manipulation of consciousness to achieve specific spiritual outcomes. It is customary to use symbols, incantations, and meditative techniques to alter ones state of awareness and access higher dimensions of reality. This aligns with the idea that "the violent take it by force," as it involves an active, intentional effort to pierce the veil of ordinary perception and connect with the divine.

Sensory deprivation, through techniques such as floatation tanks, also offers a pathway to altered states of consciousness. By removing external sensory input, the mind is free to explore its inner landscapes without distraction. This can lead to profound experiences of introspection, spiritual insight, and a sense of oneness with the universe. The mind, unencumbered by external stimuli, can become a conduit for divine experiences, aligning with Jesus' teaching that the kingdom of heaven is within us (Luke 17:21).

The biblical concept of the mind as the theater of reality is reinforced by Paul's teachings in Romans 12:2, where he urges believers to be transformed by the renewing of their minds. This transformation is an inner process, suggesting that the true kingdom of heaven is accessed through a profound internal shift. Jesus' ministry repeatedly emphasized the importance of inner transformation, urging his followers to seek the kingdom of God within themselves and to be born again in spirit.

The Esoteric Interpretation

Usually when presented with illusive passages from the bible, people either throw their hands up and say Jesus was a strange guy, or suggest a naturalistic, and albeit, lacking interpretation. I contest that without specialized occult knowledge, the kind Jesus would have had due to his time in Egypt, it would be impossible to decipher such texts. It's only when you look at the whole picture, the edges and contours of the puzzle at full brunt, that you see the dots connect. When Jesus talks about the kingdom of heaven, the Hebrew word used is shamayim meaning the domain of God and divine beings. This is the traditionally agreed meaning of heaven when Jesus says the kingdom of heaven is at hand.

The kingdom of heaven suffers violence because we are out of alignment in this world. The structures of power in this world have brainwashed us into believing we lack and are by extension disconnected from god, locked in a state irreversible without the aid of a holy man. This then is the greatest war waged on in our minds. This is the final frontier and the last great stand of the common man. Heaven then is within us. This must be true and by extension it validates itself based solely on the defense of the opposition. No one questions the existence of Santa Claus, save children. We don't entertain the trifles of foolishness less there is some deeper esoteric truth buried, and that often times done purposely.

The great teaching passed down from source to the many masters and divine teachers throughout the ages has and will forever be the kingdom of heaven is within you. You won't hear this interpretation in mainstream Abrahamic religions because it does away with the middle man. The kingdom of God is within you. So, ask yourself the natural question. What does that mean? Everything up to this point in this book was written to prepare you for this realization. This is the central nucleus of this opus. To eat of this apple means to be freed from the game, and once you have escaped your shackles you can never return. You can never be put back into the matrix once you're freed. You will have seen too much to go back. It on the one hand is a blessing and on the other the harshest of curses. This is why the journey of awakening is wrought with strife and trouble, why the world seeks to smother the fresh and fragile flame of faith.

The Forbidden Gospels

The lie has been spun for thousands of years, since the Council of Nicaea, convened in AD 325 under the rule of Emperor Constantine. This council aimed to achieve consensus in the church through the canonization of Christian doctrine. However, one of the most significant and controversial outcomes was the selection and exclusion of certain texts from the biblical canon. These decisions were driven by political motives to consolidate the church's power and maintain control over the populace by shaping the narrative of Jesus Christ and his teachings. Before the council of Nicaea, early Christianity was characterized by a diversity of beliefs and texts. Many of these texts presented interpretations of Jesus' life and teachings that differed significantly from what would later become orthodox Christianity. It can be said that the Jesus before and after the bible are two different people, one the true way of connection, and the other a pathway to isolation. The exclusion of these texts from the canonical Bible can be seen as a deliberate effort to centralize religious authority and control the spiritual narrative.

Most notable and impactful of excluded texts are the Gnostic Gospels, discovered in 1945 in Nag Hammadi, Egypt. These texts, such as the Gospel of Thomas, the Gospel of Philip, and the Gospel of Truth, portray a version of Jesus that emphasizes gnosis—personal spiritual knowledge of the divine—over vapid institutionalized worship. The Gospel of Thomas, for instance, contains sayings of Jesus that encourage direct and personal communion with the divine, suggesting that the kingdom of God is within each person. This contrasts sharply with the hierarchical and doctrinal approach of the early church, which emphasized the necessity of the church as an intermediary between God and man.

The Real Jesus

The Nag Hammadi library reveals a Jesus who is more of a mystical teacher, guiding individuals towards self-discovery and inner enlightenment, rather than a divine figure whose primary role is to be worshipped. This Gnostic perspective aligns with the idea that every person can access divine knowledge and does not need a church or priest to mediate their relationship with God. Such teachings posed a direct challenge to the emerging orthodoxy, which relied on ecclesiastical authority to interpret and dispense spiritual truths. Similarly, the Dead Sea Scrolls, discovered between 1947 and 1956 in the Qumran Caves, include texts that provide insights into early Jewish and Christian beliefs. These texts offer context about the religious landscape during the time of Jesus and suggests a variety of messianic expectations and theological ideas that diverged from what was later established as orthodox Christianity. The Scrolls underscore the diversity of early Jewish thought and the variety of interpretations about the nature of the Messiah.

The existence of apocryphal scriptures found in places like India further complicates the traditional narrative the church would have us believe. Texts such as the Gospel of Mary, which were excluded from the canonical Bible, present Mary Magdalene as a prominent disciple and a spiritual leader in her own right. This depiction challenges the patriarchal structure of the early church and suggests a more inclusive and egalitarian approach to spiritual leadership.

The removal and suppression of these texts by the Council of Nicaea can be viewed as an effort to control Christianity in a way that would unify the Roman Empire under a single, cohesive doctrine. By controlling which texts were deemed authoritative, the church could dictate the nature of Jesus' teachings and the structure of Christian practice. This consolidation of power mirrored the actions of religious leaders during Jesus' time, who sought to maintain control over spiritual matters and resist any teachings that threatened their authority.

Gnosticism, with its emphasis on direct, personal knowledge of the divine, represents a significant strand of early Christian thought that was marginalized by the orthodox church. Gnostic texts often depict Jesus as a revealer of hidden knowledge, teaching that salvation comes from within through spiritual enlightenment. This internal, individualistic approach to spirituality undermined the church's role as the gatekeeper of divine truth and posed a threat to its institutional authority.

By excluding Gnostic and other apocryphal texts, the Council of Nicaea and subsequent church leaders sought to define a uniform Christian doctrine that centralized their power. This control over spiritual knowledge ensured that the church remained the primary mediator between God and humanity, limiting individuals' direct access to the divine. The council's actions reflect a broader historical pattern of religious institutions seeking to maintain power by shaping and controlling spiritual narratives.

In essence, the decisions made at the Council of Nicaea were not merely theological but deeply political. By determining the content of the Bible and excluding texts that promoted a more personal and direct connection with God, the early church established a framework that kept the faithful reliant on ecclesiastical authority.

The Magnum Opus

Of all the things Jesus taught in the apocryphal scriptures, the core of his teachings can be reduced to what he prays in the gospel of John. His heartfelt prayer echoes the desires of the mystics throughout history. When Jesus says let us be one as we are one, he's talking about unity and connection with the council of light. As a Rabbi Jesus knew the Torah and taught the Jews of his time in accordance with what they could understand. The iconic words in Genesis, "Let us make man in our own image," is a verse directly taken from the Enuma Elish, which was written several thousand years before Genesis. Jesus, have learned the mystic arts and hidden knowledge of the Egyptians, would know this fact. Jesus himself came to show us the way, the truth, and the life. That is the way to the divine, the truth of our innate divinity, and the life of mastery and control we could have over the world.

The war is for control of your mind. If you look at the world around you you'll quickly see that everything is designed to control your mind, take hold of your thoughts, and by doing so, control your reality. You live right now with the power to abide in heaven or hell. You can do what so many before you have done and try to take the kingdom of heaven by violence, or you can apply the teachings of Jesus and all the ascended masters that came before him. You must activate your chakras, awaken your third eye, and connect with the current of the council of light.

Chapter 14

The Council of Light

This world is only as malleable as the mind that perceives it. We live as we do on this earth only because we've believed the narrative spun by those in power. There exists at this time no system or institution with sufficient power to bind or limit those who have freed their minds, having tapped into the infinite power of the universe. Thought the road to salvation is treacherous, the path must be tread. The way is well worn by those who have ventured beyond convention to discover a reality more real than this one we perceive. We all must take this journey into the unknown to truly know ourselves. What often holds us back is a lack of connection to the council of light.

In the Gospel of Matthew 6:22, Jesus states, "The light of the body is the eye: if therefore thine eye be single, thy whole body shall be full of light." This symbolically rich verse has been interpreted in various ways over the centuries. These interpretations don't take into account the occult nature of what Jesus taught, and as such will never truly grasp his intended meaning. Given what we now know about the tampering of scripture and omission of the importance of the chakra system, it's fair to conclude that Jesus is referring to the third eye in this verse. Of course, this is a concept found in many spiritual traditions, dating all the way back to the Mesopotamians. The third eye, often associated with the pineal gland in the brain, is believed to be the center of insight, intuition, and spiritual awakening in ancient cultures. Ancient texts and tablets suggest that opening the third eye through the practice of activating the chakras and raising the kundalini energy leads to enlightenment, connecting to divine energy, and accessing higher spiritual realms.

The concept of the third eye is not unique to Christianity. It appears in Hinduism, Buddhism, and the various esoteric traditions of the Sumerians and Akkadians thousands of years ago. In Hinduism, the third eye is often referred to as the ajna chakra located in the middle of the forehead. It is considered the seat of intuition and spiritual vision. Similarly, in Buddhist teachings, the third eye represents the ability to see beyond the physical world into the spiritual realm, and thus into the domain of the council of light.

Power From on High

In the Book of Acts, Jesus commands his disciples to wait in the upper room for the arrival of the Holy Spirit. This event, known as Pentecost, marks the moment when the disciples receive divine power, symbolized by tongues of fire resting upon them. The tongues of fire resting on their heads is a symbolic reference to the opening of the crown chakra, known as the thousand petal lotus, the opening of which resulted in divine communication. The "upper room" can be symbolically related to the upper part of the body, particularly the brain, where the pineal gland is located. The pineal gland, often associated with the third eye, is a small endocrine gland that has been linked to mystical and spiritual experiences.

The symbolism of God residing in his temple further supports this interpretation. In 1 Corinthians 3:16, Paul states, "Know ye not that ye are the temple of God, and that the Spirit of God dwelleth in you?" This verse suggests that the human body is a sacred vessel for divine presence. The temples of the skull, which house the brain and the pineal gland, can be seen as the inner sanctum where God resides. By activating the third eye, we open ourselves to the divine light and wisdom that dwells within us.

Throughout history, the third eye has been symbolized in various cultures. In ancient Egypt, the Eye of Horus represents protection, health, and restoration, closely linked to the concept of the third eye. In Hinduism, deities such as Shiva are often depicted with a third eye on their forehead, symbolizing their omniscience and spiritual power. Shiva is also the great destroyer of illusions. In esoteric Christianity, the third eye is sometimes referred to as the "eye of the soul," reflecting its role in spiritual perception. Evidence of the third eyes importance through history can be found in statues of pinecones and there are even depictions in Vatican City.

Scientific Methods

Though there are many spiritual practices used to activate the third eye, they often lack a foundation in scientific methodology that would provide a repeatable method of induction into higher realms. Science and spirit are meant to coexist in the journey of connection. Several scientific methods can be employed to activate the third eye and enhance its functions if used properly. It is well known in the field of neuroscience that practices such as meditation, deep breathing, and visualization are effective in stimulating the pineal gland. Research suggests that the pineal gland produces melatonin and under the right circumstances dimethyltryptamine (DMT), a compound associated with vivid dreams and mystical experiences. By focusing on the third eye during meditation, individuals can enhance their spiritual awareness and open themselves to higher states of consciousness.

Of the many scientifically tested methods of obtaining deep levels of meditation and subsequent third eye activation, there is one that I have found to be of greatest efficacy for beginners: binaural beats. Binaural beats are a widely accepted method of altering brainwave activity. This is done by playing two tones of slightly different frequencies through headphones, one in each ear. For instance, if a 200 Hz tone is played in the left ear and a 208 Hz tone in the right ear, the brain perceives a beat frequency of 8 Hz. The brain responds to this 8 Hz frequency by synchronizing its brainwaves to match this frequency, effectively guiding the listener into a theta state. They key to benefiting most from binaural beats is to use them for 30 minutes at a time on a consistent basis.

When we stay focused on the third eye and meditate upon it, after having activated the kundalini energy, we create a pathway for divine energy to flow into us. This experience is exactly what the disciples experienced when they received power from on high during Pentecost. By activating this power, we connect to the current of energy from the Council of Light. The Council of Light is a term used to describe a collective of enlightened beings who oversee and guide spiritual evolution. This council includes deities from various traditions, such as the archangels of Christianity, the gods of Hinduism, the enlightened masters of Buddhism, and the Anunnaki of the Sumerians.

The Divine Council

This divine current is what Reiki practitioners tap into when they conduct energy healings. Reiki aligns practitioners with universal life force energy. Reiki practitioners channel this energy through their hands to promote healing and balance in themselves and others. This universal energy can be seen as emanating from the Council of Light, providing divine support and guidance. By aligning with this energy, practitioners tap into a higher frequency of consciousness and facilitate spiritual growth.

The Council of Light, as described in various spiritual traditions, comprises beings of immense wisdom and power. These beings are often seen as intermediaries between the divine and humanity, providing insights, healing, and guidance. In ancient texts, such as the Vedas and the Puranas of Hinduism, deities like Vishnu and Shiva are depicted as part of a divine council that oversees the cosmos. Similarly, in Christian mysticism, the archangels Michael, Gabriel, Uriel, and Raphael are seen as members of a celestial hierarchy that guides and protects humanity.

Connecting With The Council

Connecting with the Council of Light through the activation of the third eye allows individuals to access a vast reservoir of divine knowledge and power. This connection enables the performance of magic and miracles, as described in various religious texts. For example, in the Bible, Jesus performs numerous miracles, such as healing the sick, raising the dead, and transforming water into wine. These acts are direct references to the manifestations of divine energy channeled through an open third eye and an awakened kundalini.

Throughout history, religious figures and mystics have tapped into the current of power from the Council of Light to achieve enlightenment and ascension. Figures such as the Buddha, Moses, and Rumi are examples of individuals who have connected with this divine energy and shared its wisdom with the world. The process of ascension and enlightenment involves the integration of this higher energy into the physical body, resulting in a profound transformation of consciousness. Before you can merge with higher energies, you must first be born again through the merging of your astral double.

After merging with my astral echo, I ventured on many astral journeys, being led by the echo through the astral realm. Once I was ready I was shown a door that stood open in heaven. These doorways are of great important because there are many references to what's called stargates in ancient texts and they share the contexts of teleportation to locations beyond just physically reality. In the astral realm I have found that it is impossible to travel to different realms without the guidance of the astral echo and traversal through one of these stargates. Stargates are essentially constructs that would allow for the bending or warping of space-time, creating a shortcut between two distant points in the universe. This idea is not entirely outside the realm of modern physics, as concepts like wormholes and Einstein-Rosen bridges propose similar mechanisms for traversing vast distances. In science fiction, stargates are often depicted as technological devices created by advanced civilizations, capable of generating stable and traversable portals.

Stargates and Astral Portals

The notion of traversing vast distances instantaneously has deep roots in ancient myths and legends. Various cultures speak of magical gateways or portals used by gods, demigods, and other supernatural beings to move between realms. For instance, in ancient Mesopotamian texts, the god Enki built the "Abzu," a subterranean waterway that connected the earthly realm with the divine. Similarly, in Hindu mythology, there are descriptions of "vimanas" – flying chariots used by the gods, which some ancient astronaut theorists suggest could be interpreted as advanced spacecraft or portals. Perhaps due to lack of experience, there are very few correlations made between the practice of astral projection and encounters with beings and stargates. It is my assertion that accessing these stargates requires the ability to astral travel, something the ancient mystics new the value of.

The correlation between stargates and astral travel becomes even more intriguing when considering the accounts of modern-day practitioners and psychonauts. People who have undergone deep meditation, near-death experiences, or used psychoactive substances like DMT often report encounters with beings in otherworldly realms. These experiences frequently include descriptions of passing through portals or tunnels of light, reminiscent of the stargates.

One notable aspect of these encounters is the consistent mention of advanced, non-human intelligences. These beings, often perceived as benevolent and highly knowledgeable, provide guidance and wisdom to the travelers. This aligns with ancient astronaut theories that suggest extraterrestrial beings have interacted with humanity throughout history, imparting knowledge and facilitating spiritual growth. The presence of these entities in both ancient myths and modern experiences suggests a potential link between extraterrestrial influences and the concept of stargates.

The ancient texts and artifacts provide further support for the idea of stargates as portals to other dimensions. Zecharia Sitchin, a prominent proponent of ancient astronaut theory, interprets these texts as evidence of extraterrestrial visitors who used advanced technology, including stargates, to travel between their home planet and Earth. Similarly, the biblical story of Jacob's Ladder, where Jacob dreams of a ladder reaching to heaven with angels ascending and descending, can be seen as a metaphor for the chakra system and as a stargate or portal between worlds.

My Encounter With The Council

After an intense meditation session involving an impartation of power from my astral echo, I was pulled out of body and led up into the sky. I was used to this sort of thing as it had been happening nightly for several months. I would often encounter different beings of light as I ascended into the heavens. I would watch as they delivered light orbs from heaven to earth and visa versa. I was told this was the process of prayer and manifestation conducted by angles and spirit guides. When I reached the doorway I saw it shining with a blue emanation of energy, beings of light going in and coming out of it by the hundreds. The doorway was massive.

My astral guide took me by the hand and led me through the threshold of the gateway. Passing through felt like another kind of astral projection, like I was shedding a layer of humanness or ego. This is the same thing people experience on high doses of psychedelic mushrooms. There was an immediate shift in the energy of this new place. My vision spun into a kaleidoscope of swirling energies and colors. It seemed as though I was no longer in a space. It felt more like I had entered a living environment that responded to my thoughts. It felt like I had step into the mind of a higher intelligence.

The longer I stayed in this place the more I felt a melting of who I was into the essence of the surrounding void of color and light, pulled in all directions by an intense gravity. I could hardly stand it. Once I had reached my limit and felt as though I was going to vanish completely I felt the attention of an entity in much the same way you feel someone staring at you. Fighting to maintain my permanence in this domain, I saw the face of a being form from the shifting colors of the living void, the being seeming to be a part of the void itself. Without words the being showered me with a profound sense of peace like I had never felt my whole life. I then felt a hand on my chest followed swiftly by another shifting of energy, a pulling and rushing of forces, and finally a violent shaking as I merged into a new domain. This one was filled with life, sounds, and energies. It looked to be an ancient cathedral, framed by giant pillars and what looked like living machines.

The Divine Hall

The hall I found myself in had no boundaries beyond the pillars and ancient architecture. Before me a cloud of lights appeared like eyes opening. There were hundreds of bright stars shimmering in the swirling environment. From the cloud of luminous beings a humanoid figure approached me, tall and commanding. The light of its form was blinding and simultaneously filled me with waves of overwhelming energy. Again, I felt as though I would cease to be were I to persist in this beings presence. Then I heard a voice pierce through the deep hum of the domain. It was a voice I knew my whole life but couldn't place. It seemed to emanate from everywhere, as if the void itself spoke to me. The words were heavy and terrible. "What do you want?"

Up from the core of my being bubbled a desperate plead for access. I wanted to reside in this place, this boundless expanse of light and love. I felt I was home or that a part of me was already in this place. I needed to have an open door this is domain. So that's what I asked for. The being seemed to study me and after a moment the orbs of light behind it grew brighter and a ball of light left its chest and merged with me. Just then tremendous power shot through me releasing waves of bliss and euphoria. I remained in this state of bliss until I awoke in my body.

With my eyes closed I could see the faint outline of a cord jutting out of my chest. Following that experience with the council I went on to astral project daily, traveling each time to the council of light. However, the ancient hall I had found myself in on my first visit was empty save a handful of entities. Of these, Harut, the angel mentioned in Islamic legends, and Thoth the universal scribe, made them selves known to me, offering to me astral cords. In the months that followe they taught me how to tap into the power of the omnium current and more importantly how to cleanse my energies.

With time I was given permission to share the details I have presented to you in this book. Due to my proficiency in astral traveling, I was granted the freedom to take astral cords from the various entities c the council of light and tether them to the astral bodie of people seeking divine connection. I have since called this new form of magic astral cord tethering. For those seeking connection with the council of light, as I've stated before, you'll need to connect first with your astral echo. Once you've succeeded in merges with the astral echo, you should move on to initiation into the omnium current so that you can connect with these powerful beings as I have.

Chapter 15

Connecting The Current

I've talked at great length about the dilemma that the ego creates. Namely about the nature of judgment and attachment, the removal of which will grant a sense of peace, all be it rather difficult to achieve due to our strict upbringing. So, what then is the point of these many words? If you've read this far, then surely you must believe you have gained something. And with that belief, you definitely have. The mere belief that you have learned or acquired something is enough for you to let yourself evolve. Afterall it is you at the center of it all. You are the master of the universe. To further illustrate this point, as though I need to elaborate further, think about your breath again and how it flows all on its own. See how your breath just controls itself. Take into account your heart also. It beats apart from your constant awareness of it.

It would take no great measure of faith to believe tha your breath and heartbeat are happening to you in ju the same way that the world is happening to you. See now that it is all happening to you, and at once that you are the cause of this happening. Like your heartbeat, the sun shines on you, but it is your eye th processes the light. Universal consciousness is like yo subconscious—totally you, yet operating at a higher level, undisturbed by you, as it were. You may ask yourself, as a response to this realization, what is the point of all this? That's just it, there is no point. Let that thought rummage for a moment in your mind. What if life had no point at all?

Would it be a great disaster if the only reason we wer here on this earth was to be here on this earth and merely survive. Perhaps this is all a way for the universe to answer the very same question you are asking now. Who am I? Alan Watts would suggest tha it is impossible to know yourself. Many people, including myself, used to subscribe to the idea that yo *have* to know thy self. But what is that self that you are seeking to know. Venture with me a moment longer. Have you ever asked yourself why you are curious to know who you are? And after asking that have you asked why to even that?

The Nature of Reality

When I was much younger, a friend introduced me to the 'why' game. In so doing he thought he'd be leading me back to god as the great answer for everything. Though I didn't take him seriously then, the game stuck with me. I would often find myself wondering vhy. Just why. Why do I hurt? Why do I strive to be ;reat? Why, God, Why? So many questions I would ask ;od or the universe or whoever or whatever you think s holding the keys. I would beg for answers as if inswers would make me feel any better. Eventually I igured out that It wasn't answers I wanted. It was beace. And somehow along the way we were made to believe that answers and peace were the same thing. 'm here to tell you they are not. Not even close. No amount of head knowledge about the workings of this eality will suffice to service to you peace. peace is equanimity in all situations, regardless of the answers being given. That is freedom—not having to choose or vant or need or strive. Freedom is peace from obligation or guilt. Freedom is living unafraid. It is accepting who you are and understanding you are more and you are nothing all at the same time. Freedom is etting go of the need to know what or why. Though it's good to ask why. I find that it works similarly to the Buddhist poem that only has the purpose of showing you that you can't figure it out; that despite your craftiness you can't solve the riddle of your existence.

That happens simply because you are existence tself. And just like a fire cannot burn itself, or a knife cannot cut itself, so too you cannot know yourself. Wherever you point you will only find yourself. Like our meditations from earlier in this book. Once you quiet the mind by observing the outer world and then the inner world, you realize they are one and the same. You see there is no boundary between your thoughts and the music of the natural world around you. You see that you are not the act of listening alone but you are also the object of listening. You are the experience and the experiencer, the canvas and the painter. Both require the other for the experience to be had.

It is impossible to see the fabric of reality through this lens and not see oneself woven into the tapestry, just as connected as everything else. So, what is meant by the phrase "who am I,"? I believe it is the question that drives us to persist. It's why this game of life was switched on in the first place. At this very moment, I am connected to you. In fact, you can just as easily connect with anyone. Simply by closing your eyes and allowing yourself to zoom out, you would immediately see that you are not a finger, but the whole hand that it is attached to.

Set your intention to explore what is, to be present for this unfolding of time, this crescendo of events. Try to live a life apart from judgment. Just observe, and even observe passively as well. Don't assume, as many people do when accepting this pursuit of divine connection, that meditation is going to help you level up. If anything, the more you abandon that idea the sooner you will see change in yourself. Approach your spiritual life in the same way you do breathing. Do it while also knowing it is a happening. You have to learn to dance alone and in so doing you'll realize you are dancing with God.

Awakening the Inner God

You stand now in the foyer of a massive house. So massive that you can't see where the house ends or begins. Within this house there are many doors, each one leading to a new adventure, a new glimpse into the ıemory of who you are. So, what then is the path to onnection with God? Why that's simple. Make a fist. 'ou can't fit much in that clenched fist if anything at ll. Now open your hand. Now you can hold practically nything. So, be open and unclutched. You've searched ɔr long enough. Enlightenment is here and always has een. God has been watching the play of your life hrough your eyes. God has been listening to the music ou love with your ears and feeling the range of your motions with your heart. The path to connection has een within you all along just waiting to be activated. 'he path to connection with the divine is awareness; he very thing you've always had and always will have. ook to your awareness, and there too you will find bundant spiritual freedom and abiding nlightenment.

Ve all have within us the power of creation because we re connected to source. Many call this connection God's love, and others call it love and light or Christ onsciousness. Far fewer people know how to activate t. It's one thing to experiences this energy pontaneously, but another thing entirely to tap into his power at will. The material in this book was vritten in such a way to help you tap into this power ıaturally. You've felt this energy if you've listened to nusic that moved you or saw a painting that inspired ou. This energy causes goosebumps and chills to flow hrough the body. The scientific community calls this rission. Everyone has felt this at one point or another. Frission is often associated with emotional states and ntense spiritual experiences.

Recent scientific research has begun to uncover the physiological and neurological underpinnings of these chills, linking them to increased electrical potential in the brain and heightened brainwave activity. Scientif studies have shown that spiritual chills are associate with the brain's reward system. When individuals experience these chills, there is a significant increase activity within the nucleus accumbens, a region of the brain involved in the release of dopamine, the neurotransmitter responsible for pleasure and reward This heightened activity is often accompanied by a sense of euphoria or a profound emotional response, which can explain the chills experienced during religious or spiritual events. Research published in th journal *Social Cognitive and Affective Neuroscience* demonstrated that people who experience chills when listening to music exhibit increased functional connectivity between the auditory cortex and the emotional processing areas of the brain, such as the anterior insular cortex and the ventromedial prefront cortex.

The Divine Design

Additionally, these chills are linked with an increase i brainwave activity, particularly in the alpha and thet wave frequencies. Alpha waves are associated with relaxed, meditative states, while theta waves are linked to deep relaxation and creative insights. The surge in these brainwave frequencies during moments of spiritual chills suggests a state of heightened awareness and openness, which aligns with descriptions of religious euphoria and deep spiritual experiences. This increased electrical potential in the brain during such moments has been observed through electroencephalogram studies, which show heightened brainwave patterns correlating with the intensity of the chills. These studies suggest we have a profound ability to alter our perception of reality. Connecting to this current of power opens the door of our true godly potential.

Traditionally, the induction of chills is considered a function of the sympathetic nervous system, which controls the body's involuntary responses, such as the fight-or-flight response. Because of this, it has been widely believed that controlling or inducing chills at will is *impossible*. However, recent research has identified individuals who can induce these chills at will, challenging the conventional understanding of the sympathetic nervous system's control.

A study published in the journal *Consciousness and Cognition* explored the abilities of people who could self-induce chills. These individuals reported a greater sense of control over their emotional states and a heightened ability to experience profound moments of connection, both spiritually and emotionally. The study found that these individuals had a unique capacity to focus their attention and manipulate their physiological state to induce chills, suggesting a higher level of mind-body connectivity.

These chills have also been linked to kundalini awakening. The experience of spiritual chills during a kundalini awakening aligns with the descriptions of energy surges and profound shifts in consciousness reported by practitioners. The ability to induce chills at will may indicate an advanced state of spiritual development, where one has greater control over the flow of this energy within the body.

Further adding to the scientific understanding of Frisson are the magnetite crystals found in the human brain. Magnetite is a naturally occurring mineral with magnetic properties. It is believed to play a role in the brain's response to electromagnetic fields. The pineal gland, often referred to as the "third eye" in spiritual traditions, contains these magnetite crystals and is thought to be sensitive to electromagnetic activity.

Now, this is the interesting part. This is what has been hidden from us since the days of the Egyptians. When spiritual chills are induced, the pineal gland creates a piezoelectric effect due to the mechanical pressure exerted by the chills. This effect, where mechanical stress generates an electrical charge, can result in the production of an electromagnetic field within the brain. The electromagnetic field generated by the pineal gland during these moments of chills opens the door to the divine and higher states of consciousness.

Pentecost in The Present

The conscious control of this energy is the heart of magic and the journey of the spiritual seeker. This energy is connection with the divine aspect. Most people only experience seconds of this state, which doesn't do very much to activate the piezoelectric effect of the pineal gland. Several chapters ago I talked about the disciples on the day of Pentecost when they received power from on high. Jesus instructing them to wait in the upper room can be interpreted as maintaining the state of connection or the chills. If you're able to maintain the chills for 5 to 10 minutes you will receive power from on high. This often leads to spontaneous astral projection, activation of the light body, and even transcendence from this reality completely. Maintaining this state takes practice but is rather simple to learn. In just about every mystic tradition the importance of devotion and worship is stressed. The reason for that is the development of the ability to induce the chills at will. The vibration of love opens the heart chakra allowing for the energy to flow. Focusing on love is the first of two parts of the most effective method.

The voice is the second element of activation. Since antiquity magicians have been using words with magic properties because they understood that reality was the product of sound vibration and frequency. The vibration of words has been known to unlock latent power within the body. During my time with the omnium nexus I was taught to use certain words that have an effect over the spiritual realm, thus causing change to the physical. The use of sacred names to alter reality dates back to the time of the Mesopotamians, gaining traction and widespread use in Egyptian magical practice. They believed that the calling of deities and the use of incantations could induce heightened states of awareness. In more modern times divine names are used in Islamic magic and occult circles. Hindu yogis would call the names of the chakras to open them. This suggests that when love is built up in your heart, raising your vibration, the words of power act as the spark that light the fire of energy in the body.

The names I was given carried with them specific instructions for their use. Things like the number of repetitions and on which days to recite them. After receiving these names, I tested them on myself with great effect. So, I presented them to a close friend I had known for years. I presented the idea to him and assured him of the simplicity and effectiveness. After an hour of sharing with him the names he called me back panting and hysteric. Never before had he felt chills so powerfully and for so long, he said. He said it was like waves of static rolling over his body. He raved about seeing a glowing being in his house. He had opened the divine door in his mind, allowing him to peer beyond the veil. I have since given those names to hundreds of people who all have similar experiences of instant connection and a sense of abounding love and acceptance from the universe.

The words I present to you below are most powerful when met with your faith and strong desire. It isn't enough to simply repeat the words, you must feel them bringing your inner being to life and connecting you with a current of power that is your birth right to experience. You must feel and know that you are connecting with source consciousness and becoming one with love and light. You don't need anything to make these names work but faith and clear intention.

To start find a quiet place where you won't be disturbed and play whatever music helps you to become aware of love stirring up within you. For me this is worship music, but all kinds of music have worked for people in the past. Some practitioners have even taken to singing or playing an instrument before or during the recitation. Once you are comfortable and have picked the music you want to listen to, become aware of your breathing and relax your body for several minutes. When you feel deeply relaxed begin to chant the names below for the given number of times. When you say the names you must vibrate them as a monk would vibrate the word OM while meditating. You should feel the vibration in the center of your chest while you do this. Don't rush through the recitation and trust your intuition for proper pronunciation. Be present and open. You may feel the need to say the names quickly at times and slower at others. Go with the flow and find the current.

Power Awakening Incantation

Incantation:

"Tamirah Shalom Vedeh Roshai,

Kalah Nedar Vior Selah Veshim."

Recitations: 21 times

Instructions: Recite this incantation to heighten your intuitive and psychic abilities, allowing you to sense energies and foresee outcomes with greater accuracy.

Omnium Current Initiation Ritual

This ritual is for initiation into the Omnium Current of Magic, invoking protection and guidance from the archangels and connecting with the divine energies of Shiva, Odin, and Thoth from the Omnium Nexus. This is a powerful energetic shift that should only be done after you have done the meditations given earlier in this book and your energy has been awakened with the Inner Power Awakening Incantation. This ritual is more advanced and can result in the physical manifestation of sounds, light, energy and spirits.

Preparation:

- **Location:** A quiet, sacred space where you will not be disturbed.
- **Materials:**
  - Four candles (one for each cardinal direction: east, south, west, north).
  - Incense (preferably frankincense or sandalwood).
  - A small bowl of water.
  - A bowl of salt.
  - A representation of each deity (e.g., images or statues of Shiva, Odin, and Thoth).
  - A ceremonial robe or specific attire for the ritual.
  - A bell or chime. (Simply clap your hands or snap your fingers if you don't have a bell)

    - A ceremonial dagger or athame for drawing the circle. (You can use your hand or finger if you don't have an athame)

Ritual Steps:

- **Purification:**
    - Light the incense and let the smoke purify the space.
    - Sprinkle salt in a circle around the area.
    - Place the candles at the cardinal points: east (yellow), south (red), west (blue), and north (green).
- **Creating the Magic Circle:**
    - Stand in the center of the space with the ceremonial dagger.
    - Point the dagger at the ground and slowly rotate clockwise, visualizing a protective circle of light forming around you.
    - Say: "By the power of the Omnium Current and the light within, I create this sacred circle, a space between worlds."
- **Invocation of the Archangels:**
    - Facing east, light the yellow candle and say: "I call upon Archangel Raphael, guardian of the east, bringer of air and healing. Protect this circle."
    - Facing south, light the red candle and say: "I call upon Archangel Michael, guardian of the south, bringer of fire and courage. Protect this circle."
    - Facing west, light the blue candle and say: "I call upon Archangel Gabriel, guardian

    - of the west, bringer of water and communication. Protect this circle."
    - Facing north, light the green candle and say: "I call upon Archangel Uriel, guardian of the north, bringer of earth and wisdom. Protect this circle."
- **Centering and Grounding:**
    - Stand in the center of the circle, hold your hands over the bowl of water, and say: "Water of life, connect me to the flow of the Omnium Current."
    - Dip your fingers into the water and touch your forehead, heart, and hands, visualizing the energy flowing into you.
- **Calling the Omnium Nexus:**
    - Light the central incense or candle (if not already lit) and stand before the representations of Shiva, Odin, and Thoth.
    - Say: "I call upon the Omnium Nexus, the divine Council of Light, to witness this initiation. I invoke thee, Shiva, lord of transformation and cosmic dance. I invoke thee, Odin, seeker of wisdom and keeper of runes. I invoke thee, Thoth, master of knowledge and scribe of the gods. Guide me in the ways of the Omnium Current, and let your energies flow through me."
- **Affirmation and Oath:**
    - Place your hand over your heart and recite: "I, [name], stand before the Omnium Nexus, pledging my dedication to the path of light and wisdom. I vow to honor the teachings of Shiva, Odin, and Thoth, to uphold the principles of the

Omnium Current, and to seek truth and enlightenment in all my endeavors."

- **Closing the Circle:**
  - Thank the deities: "Thank you, Shiva, Odin, and Thoth, for your presence and guidance. May your light continue to shine upon my path."
  - Thank the archangels, extinguishing each candle as you go: "Thank you, Raphael; thank you, Michael; thank you, Gabriel; thank you, Uriel."
  - Use the dagger to symbolically cut through the circle, saying: "I release this circle, but its protection and energy remain with me. So mote it be."
- **Integration:**
  - Sit quietly for a few minutes, meditating on the energies you have invoked and feeling the connection with the Omnium Current.
  - Ring the bell or chime to signal the end of the ritual.

Post-Ritual Reflection:

- Keep a journal to record your experiences during the ritual, any visions, feelings, or messages received.
- Continue to meditate daily on the energies of Shiva, Odin, and Thoth, and practice visualizing the flow of the Omnium Current within you.

By performing this initiation ritual, you align yourself with the ancient energies and wisdom of the Omnium

Nexus, opening the path to deeper understanding and mastery of the magical arts. This sacred practice connects you with a lineage of divine knowledge, empowering you to carry forward the teachings of the great deities and the light of the Omnium Current.

Having reached the end of this book, tested your mind with the mysteries and challenges presented by the truth, you now stand ready to enter the heaven within you and walk in the power of the ancient mystics who came before you. The purpose of this work is to help you connect to the powers that exist all around you. This book serves as an invitation for your desires and aspirations to manifest into this reality and help you to achieve a state of lasting enlightenment. I encourage you to email me with questions or concerns pertaining to your spiritual journey, as I am always open to help. Join the Facebook group: Astral Mind Foundation and visit the website www.astralmindfoundation.com for more information about astral cord tethering and the different spirits of the omnium nexus.

Blessings

Love and Light

Namaste

And as always

Never Stop Adventuring